THE AUTHOR STUCK LIST

THE AUTHOR STUCK LIST

Better-Faster Author Success

Book 1

BECCA SYME

Hummingbird Books

For the Better-Faster Academy coaches and staff.

I wouldn't want to do this job without you.

PART I
INDIVIDUALIZED AUTHOR PROCESSES

I got stuck writing this book. (I know. Right?) And like I often do, I phoned a friend to chat through the slow-down and they asked me, "What are you hoping will happen with this book?"

I laughed, of course, because my hopes for books are nothing if not ambitious.

"I want to make it possible for every author to get unstuck at any time in any book they're writing, ever."

And of course, my friend laughed at that because... why not shoot for the moon, Becca? But also, it helped me to get unstuck because I know that's not possible. Logically, I know it.

How do I know it for sure? Because I've coached 6000 individual authors (not groups of authors, either... one-on-one coaching for 45 minutes or more), and I know the stuck-ness is sometimes complicated by additional factors. Those factors, I'll never be able to do anything about with a book. But hopefully those people will know to either come find a coach or go to a therapist, and then I can move on to helping the people I can help.

Expectations are one of several factors of being stuck, as writers. But the other factors are much easier to work through on our own. That's the goal of this book:

To provide a comprehensive tool to deal with manuscript and process stuck-ness in a way that can be customized to you and to your process.

Why customization?

Let me get nerdy for a second here.

If you've ever been part of a research study in the past, either in the creation of the study or as a research participant, you may be familiar with the concept of statistical significance. If the findings of research are statistically significant, that means the findings pass the reasonable doubt of random chance.

Reasonable doubt of random chance.

Essentially, is my hypothesis correct? Is there no doubt that randomness can't explain the results?

What it does *not* mean, however, is that the results are 100% applicable. Let's take one example.

I have a brown-haired friend named Daniel. I meet another brown-haired Daniel and suddenly, I wonder... do all people named Daniel have brown hair? Let's do a random sample of Daniels because two could still be random.

Could ten be random?

What about 100?

The higher the number, the less likely the pattern would break only because of additional numbers added to the sample. But what does the data mean?

Does it mean all brown-haired babies must be named Daniel? No. All it takes is a quick sample of babies in my extended family (five out of twenty-three have brown hair, none of them are named Daniel) to know that's not predictive.

But it still doesn't mean that all Daniels must have brown hair. Because in a sample, you're still going to find Daniel-named babies who have non-brown hair.

So we know that Factor A (the name of Daniel) does not predict Factor B (brown hair), but we've also found B does not predict A. So what relevance does the data have? There is a more-likely-than-not chance that a baby named Daniel will have brown hair.

(This is completely made-up data, by the way. I have not conducted this research. Nor should you.)

(And if you just decided you would do the research because I told you not to... I see you.)

The problem with statistical significance is: the data itself doesn't tell you anything predictive. Because the data can't get at the *why* behind why the numbers exist. That's up to the researchers to interpret.

An ethical researcher might say that the results of the brown-haired Daniel study showed a correlation between the name Daniel and having brown hair. An unethical researcher would draw a conclusion that all babies named Daniel will have brown hair.

We laugh at that, and we say, "That would never happen," because we instinctively know those two factors are not predictive of each other. Many of us have named babies before. No one is looking at a baby's hair color and saying, "There's the brown hair, so the name must be Daniel." We know that's ridiculous.

But when it comes to particular behaviors in our author career, we throw those correlation/causation thoughts out the window. We hear someone say, "You should outline so you never get stuck" and we assume, "If I'm getting stuck, there's something wrong with me" and we start outlining. Only to keep getting stuck.

The problem with most author advice is that it assumes causation that isn't true. It sees a brown-haired baby and wants to predict the name will be Daniel. But in the same way that all parents choose baby names for their own reasons, authors get stuck in their process for their own reasons.

This book will attempt to help uncover the individualized reason, diagnose the stuck-ness, and then apply a fix for that stuck-ness.

The key word is: individualized.

We make no assumptions about why you are stuck. We ask questions, we look at the answers, and find the application.

I specifically made this tool to be used in a different way with each person, and with different results.

And if there's nothing in these pages that will help, please find a real live person to support you because you may have expectations that need to be realigned, like I did, or you may need a therapist to help uncouple the fear from your process.

There will be a companion workbook available, for those who want to have a print book to work through, but the goal is that this book can be used on its own.

Ok, let's get into the process of consistently getting unstuck.

ONE

The Tool

___

YOU ARE A TOOL.

(If you were born before the year 2000, that sounds like an insult, but I don't mean "you're an idiot." I mean, in the toolbox of life, we are all different tools. And you, dear writer, are a specific type of tool with a very particular set of skills.)

If you heard Liam Neeson's voice there, ten points.

But on a more serious note, most of us have had the experience of picking up a craft book, looking for the silver bullet, and walking away frustrated. We wonder why this famous writer's (or famous productivity guru's) advice doesn't work for us.

The reason is, they're a tool.

But not the same kind of tool as you.

So the instruction manual for their tool type isn't going to work for your tool type. Yet somehow, we expect it will, and we operate in our writing world as though every single craft book is for us.

This is the reason, by the way, why a lot of us get stuck so regularly. We're using instruction manuals for someone else's tool. We're trying to use a screwdriver to hammer a nail. It's sort of working, but our handle keeps breaking because it wasn't made for this kind of brute force.

But we've been doing the "good student" thing and learning from everyone. The reason I do this work is because I started off as a fiction writer who had a very particular set of skills. I watched my friends struggle to find their process among an overabundance of information, workshops, books, advice, and conferences. Yet they still struggled.

The skills I'd been taught—by using the CliftonStrengths© development program—made me instinctively reject advice that wasn't made for my type of tool. But my friends weren't able to as quickly say, "Not for me" when they would learn something.

I had friends who were natural discovery writers trying to outline because they'd been told they had to. I watched friends who were extremely private and introverted putting themselves on social media because they'd been told all writers needed a social platform.

It was painful to watch.

Not because of their struggle. Struggle can be really beneficial. But because they were trying to do something they were never going to succeed at, on the levels they needed to succeed at. Plus, they were ignoring assets they already had because they were told those assets were weaknesses.

So I started trying to help writers discover what type of tool they were, and because I'd already been doing it in other arenas for so long, it became second nature. And that work is what led me to this place.

In my career, individually coaching authors for success alignment, I've noticed that there are major patterns to how things happen in our author career. How our personality and/or environment and/or assets and/or systems can impact our success. My life's work has been to offer individual guidance. But when it comes to helping a broader base of authors, I realized something.

The patterns are often big-picture enough to be helpful to people, even outside the coaching setting. So this book is based on four major premises.

1. We're all very different. And those differences matter.

That means:

2. Not everyone gets stuck for the same reason. The cause ("why") is different for each writer (and sometimes, each situation).

That means:

3. We can't all get unstuck in the same way, but there are still patterns to how the majority of us get stuck if we can align ourselves to the *why* of the stuck.

Hence, this tool.

If we can figure out *why* you are getting stuck (especially the stuck-ness that happens consistently), we can more consistently get you unstuck. Not just theoretically, but actually.

We do find it helpful, in our coaching practice, to use the CliftonStrengths© metric as a way of understanding how our brain functions, but any level of self-awareness should help this process.

Do you know whether or not you are externally motivated?

Do you know whether or not your brain needs thinking time in order to reach clarity?

Do you know whether or not your need for constant forward motion is a barrier to slow downs?

(Not everyone will resonate with all of these. Again. Different tools.)

But if you don't have any current level of self-awareness about your personality or how your brain functions, I'm going to recommend that you do some kind of reliable assessment to get a sense for where you fall on some of these continuums. It's not 100% necessary (I do think self-assessment can still be valuable even without tools), but when I talk about the need for thinking to clarity, or talk about the need to move at a faster pace, having some kind of metric can be helpful. There are several tools out there. If you don't like the Strengths, find one that works for you.

This process will go much easier if you have a level of self-awareness about what you need from the process of writing.

That being said, let's assume you have it so we can progress. Because I really want to get into the meat and potatoes of this book.

The Stuck List Tool Kit.

TWO

The Tool Kit

THIS TOOL KIT WAS ORIGINALLY CREATED AS A card deck and a workbook. But when I sat down to write this book, I wanted to take the information from both the card deck and the workbook and create a tool kit that could be used with or without the deck.

The goal is for you to be able to use this book as a stand-in if you don't have (or don't want) the card deck. This book should be fully usable on its own. Each of the sections will expand on the advice from the deck and explain how to customize this tool for yourself.

When I created the deck, the goal was to be able to sort through the cards to find the ones that would most consistently work to get you unstuck, and then keep those cards beside you at your computer or in your purse when you went to the coffee shop so you'd always have the ability to take action quickly when you get stuck.

One of the most frustrating parts of being a writer is not being able to quickly diagnose when the stuck is happening so we can keep making progress. So the goal of the deck was to have something handy where the "get you unstuck" could be quick. Alleviate some of that pain.

Because there are different reasons *why* we are stuck, and each of those reasons tends to have different fixes, I also needed to organize the advice and information into those diagnoses. So I came up with six major patterns of stuck that emerged from the data I had collected from coaching.

1. Needing Clarity
2. Getting Bored
3. Inability to Progress
4. Emotional Discord
5. Environmental Block
6. Lack of Information

There are, of course, more technical "reasons" why stuck-ness might happen, but most whys fit into one of these six areas.

Each of those "reasons" got its own domain color for the card deck, and then in addition to that, some of the advice will work to fix multiple different "why" problems. So I also created icons for each of the domains of stuck, and whenever a piece of advice works for more than one, I added that icon onto the card itself.

Here's an example:

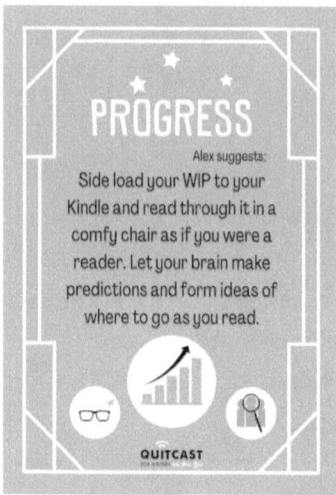

We ran a Kickstarter to launch this card deck, and one of the levels was the opportunity to add your advice into the deck. I appreciated everyone who gave these advice cards because each of them was a different action than I already had in the deck.

This piece of advice was, "Side load your WIP to your Kindle and read through it in a comfy chair as if you were a reader. Let your brain make predictions and form ideas of where to go as you read."

The domain of "Progress" is about things we often don't consider progress because they aren't "getting words on the page," but which are really necessary to the creation of stories. So I put this advice into the Progress domain because this "reading the book back as a reader" is really necessary for some of us to get unstuck, but we often resist it. So it was a perfect fit for the Progress domain.

But it also represents the "Clarity" domain, where we often need to let our brains process things in a different way in order to reach clarity, so I added the glasses icon to represent that domain. And then the Kindle side-load also represents grabbing a "Resource" that isn't the computer, so I added that one as well.

One piece of advice, potentially solving three different types of problems. So each piece of advice in the deck has the potential to be in more than one domain of helpfulness.

As we go through this book, I will outline the work from the Tool Kit workbook you'll need to know in order to use the tool kit, and then we'll go through each of the pieces of advice individually.

Let's start off with the domains themselves.

THREE

The Six Categories of Stuck

CLARITY
The need for specific or complete thought

THIS IS OFTEN A PERSONALITY TRAIT. THE need or desire to have clarity before you progress. It can come from many different places, so let's focus on how it manifests.

A lack of clarity will feel like blurriness or confusion. "I'm not sure what happens next" or "I'm not sure what they will do here" is the most common manifestation of this type.

Most of us who struggle with a lack of clarity at different points in the book will struggle every book, and often in the same places each story. It's common, for instance, for 50% of the way through the book to be a stoppage point.

The need for clarity in the story often won't be the only "let me think on this more" experience in the writer's life. In fact, they will almost always have some kind of internal need to process and understand. So the certainty-seeking will resonate outside of their writing life as well.

When you regularly need to stop and think, there can be a lot of trauma around the process—not helped by the fact that most of the writing teachers in the world consider thinking to be antithetical to writing, which honestly blows my mind. Thinking is what produces writing. Finding clarity, especially for people who are wired to seek it, is the most productive creative activity.

So this category is one-part validation of process, and one part QTP (question the premise)[1] because a lot of us have been taught *not* to think, when thinking is what we need the most.

In fact, some of us get stuck primarily because we refuse to allow ourselves the thinking time or processing time we need. For those writers, the majority of the Clarity domain in this deck will be comprised of things your intuition is telling you to do, but the writing gurus have told you not to.

Ignore the writing gurus when their advice doesn't work. Our brains are all very different and those differences matter as to what advice we can and can't take. If you need clarity, you have to seek it.

This domain will attempt to provide action steps for seeking clarity.

EMOTION
Emotional discord or confusion

I ALMOST CALLED THIS ONE "EMOTIONAL damage," but I wasn't sure the TikTok fans would read this book en masse. And also, "damage" is a bit extreme for what happens in this version of stuck-ness.

When we are wired to be emotionally responsive to other people, that will often become a source of being stuck in our manuscripts. For a few reasons.

First, people who are wired to respond to emotions also feel their characters' feelings as though the events were happening to real people. This is something I've found that writers tend not to like to talk about. They feel very vulnerable admitting this, so it tends not to get said from workshop stages. But it's a significant portion of stuck-ness in writing.

In fact, when I first started regularly coaching writers in their processes, I found this phenomenon happening so often, I considered doing a course just on this trait alone. The number of writers I coached who would regularly get stuck when their characters were suffering was significant.

And of course, some of you are being judgmental right now. That is also why it doesn't get talked about from workshop stages or in the pages of nonfiction books. Because half of writers are critical about this state of being.

It's also why emotion-sensitive (or emotion-intuitive) writers tend not to be aware of this problem for themselves. They often try not to admit to other writers that they feel this way. "It sounds crazy" is the most common phrasing I heard around this.

But it's not crazy at all. In fact, it's the most normal thing ever, for writers who are wired to be emotionally responsive. Rather than trying to change the wiring, or trying to develop the ability to isolate yourself from the emotions... how about we just accept the fact that emotions of everyone are deeply impactful, and work with it?

The second reason emotionally responsive people get stuck is the plethora of emotionally damaging things that can happen in the world around us. Either to family/friends, or to strangers. It doesn't make a difference whether the emotions are near or far. It matters if someone is feeling them.

This is why I often encourage people who are wired for emotional responsiveness to stay off the internet in the morning. No need to introduce additional emotions into the mix. (And again, that's assuming you're writing in the morning, which not all of us do.) When you like helping others process their emotions (or you don't like it, but you're capable of it, so you do it anyway), it comes with a price. And that price is often your own productivity.

No judgment. We're all completely different. It's just important to know that no behavior is cost-free. Every behavior has a price—who pays the price is the question.

The third reason emotionally responsive people often get stuck is the confusion about the direction of the narrative. Emotional arcs. One of the core traits of emotionally responsive people is the ability to know what other people are feeling. This doesn't always come with the ability to name the emotions, though. In fact, it often comes intuitively and then requires a response, rather than understanding, so it's not uncommon for these types of writers to be reacting to emotions without knowing what they are.

The upside of that is you'll always be trying to respond to people as they really are, instead of what they say they are (which are almost always different). The downside is, characters are people too, only they won't move along in their actions until you understand them. So some of these stuck causes will require some clarity-seeking (so they'll have overlap with the Clarity domain).

ENVIRONMENT
Environmental blockage or impact

WHEN I FIRST STARTED COACHING WRITERS, I was surprised at how often the following scenario would happen:

A writer would come to me, frustrated that they were stuck. I would ask about how their life was going, and they kept trying to return to the book.

"No," I'd say. "We'll get to the book. Tell me about what's going on in your life."

A little put out, they'd finally talk about what was happening in their life, and it was almost always a big impact. Moving across the country, major illness diagnoses, family members or friends in crisis, house fires, etc.

In my head, I was thinking, "It's not the book, Jessica. It's your life." But I couldn't say that out loud, of course, because they were also often in crisis. Gently, I'd ask why they expected themselves to be able to write, whether or not there was stability in their life.

Their answer would always be, "Well, X writer finished their novel while their husband had cancer."

And without invalidating that other writer's experience, I would have to say, "Is that a realistic expectation to hold for yourself?"

When your environment matters to your productivity (including the events surrounding your life), it matters. So the goal then becomes to fix or change the environment, rather than trying to develop skills for compartmentalization that we don't have.

To be fair, you can still develop the skills for compartmentalization if you want (or try to), but it's going to be faster to fix or deal with the environmental instability. And again, sometimes, the development of those skills won't actually work because it conflicts with some bedrock formation of your personality.

If it sounds like I'm somehow advocating we never grow or change, I'm definitely not. A core part of our work (especially with Strengths) is to grow and change. But there's a difference between acquiring skills with no resistance and acquiring skills with decades of resistance. When you're naturally wired to want to compartmentalize, it seems easy to develop the skills further. When you are not naturally wired that way, it's a mammoth task that may or may not have the right outcome.

For instance, a lot of the well-meaning advice in writing groups in this arena boils down to "Just stop caring." But the advice-giver doesn't realize just how many supportive skills they have acquired over the years that allow them to not care. The person who does care, however, has also developed a net of supportive skills that make them want to care. It isn't simply possible to just stop caring when you have decades (and decades, sometimes) of skill development in the opposite direction.

In fact, this type of situation is exactly the illustration of why 95% of adult behavioral change never happens. Because we fail to give credence to just how voracious the patterns in our brain are, and how much work it takes to change them.

If you were to open up the brain of an environmentally responsive person, you would find clusters of firing neurons that are triggering skills to preserve and protect all those responsive traits. Not just a button that says, "caring about X" that could be turned off. But when you already have those clusters of supportive behaviors, it feels like there's just a button you can turn off.

There's no button.

You have to unlearn and relearn sets of skills. It's massive internal work and it's often called "reparenting" work. Think of how long it takes to parent someone. That's the kind of work we're talking about here. It can be intensive.

This is why I say things like, "Don't try to change these traits, just work with them." Because change is possible, but it's dependent on how much reparenting work has to happen. Or how much skill development needs doing.

Honestly, we don't have time to do that, sometimes. We just need to manage the environment instead.

So as much as I wish I could look at those people who told me, "Well, X writer can finish a novel in the ER," and tell them, "Just stop caring," I know from years of experience, it won't work. And these pieces of environmental stability advice won't be necessary for everyone. But when you need them, they're there for you.

And we really need to stop judging each other, as writers. It's the least helpful thing we do. When people are differently wired from us, we just need to accept it and let them live their lives. Judgment doesn't help anyone.

Anyway, you can see this conversation touched a nerve with me. It's the reason I can't go into writer's groups on Facebook anymore or watch writers give advice on Twitter or TikTok. I just can't take the way we judge each other without first trying to empathize. If we could just believe people when they say, "This is how it is for me," and lead with empathy first, rather than judgment... the writing world would be a significantly better place.

But let me say one last thing about the "environmental blockage or impact" area. If you are wired to need stability in your environment, there's a good chance this kind of judgment has been part of your whole life, and you might be resistant to reading that segment of the book for that reason alone.

If you are in that place, I'm going to ask you to read it with curiosity, rather than a search for mandate. Read it as though you were wanting to help a friend with their stuckness, rather than fix your own. That objectivity can almost always help the blows to land easier if they're there to land.

And also, as someone who has some of this wiring, I can tell you, this wiring is a gift to the world. So we might as well make it a gift to ourselves, also, and protect it.

I recently moved across the country to protect the impact of environment on my creativity. It was costly and painful. But the way I feel in the new environment is a freedom I'd like to bottle and sell. That's how powerful it can be when we align parts of ourselves and how we are wired with the correct actions.

Freedom.

. . .

PROGRESS
Inability to progress with word count

BECAUSE WORD COUNT IS TRACKABLE (OR "page count" if you were publishing traditionally before 2010), we often get sucked into the idea that progress equals more words or pages. In fact, it's common for coaching calls to be reports of numbers from days where the writer felt "most productive" and the numbers from days where they felt "unproductive."

But when we dig deeper into the things they did to support the writing, we find that they were still making progress. Just not in the amount of words written. But the actual process of the book was progressing.

There is a lot of unhelpful rhetoric around this mindset in the writing community, where we hear things like, "You can't sell a book you haven't written" and "You can't edit a blank page." While the first sentence is at least objectively true (the second sentence isn't, by the way[2]), neither of those are helpful when you consider how many things often need to happen that aren't writing in order to complete a novel, screenplay, or piece of writing.

In fact, we usually use the "miles on a highway" metaphor to visualize this with clients. If you imagine that there are 300 miles to drive/walk between conception of the idea of a book and the completion of that book, each mile has two rules.

1. They must be done in order. (You can't run mile 44 before you run mile 2.)

2. They are all necessary. (You can't select which miles you're going to run and which ones you're going to skip.)

What I don't mean is that everyone should write chronologically, of course. If your book happens to be written out of order, but you have to write those scenes in the order they come to you, then you are still running/driving those miles of the novel in order, just not the chapters in order.

The "in order" part is important because some of us need to do non-writing activities in order to generate writing activities. We have to think in order to write. Or we have to research in order to write.

If all the writing miles are purple and all the researching miles are green and all the marketing miles are blue and all the editing miles are black, many of us have deep seated beliefs about how those miles "should" be driven. We instinctively prefer all the miles between 1 and 300 to be purple writing miles.

When our brain wants us to do a different color, we get frustrated with it. Some part of us considers all those other colors to be an exit off the productivity highway, rather than seeing that they are all productive in that they are all necessary to complete the novel.

We would rather only writing miles existed. (Often.)

But these miles in the novel progress must be done in order. If you have to research in order to write, then you have to. Trying to drive that purple mile at 44 before you drive the green miles of 42 and 43 is only going to mean it takes longer to get to 44.

It is **not** going to make 42 and 43 go away.

Many of the progress cards in this deck are reminders that we have to do the activities in the order our brain requires them.

One of the ways I hope writers will use this tool is to pull their most common methods of getting unstuck and leave them on their desk so they can jump more quickly into progress, rather than being frustrated with having to drive miles they don't want to drive.

If we want to finish the novel, we have to drive those miles in order. Might as well just take action on them more quickly. Save us the time of looking for ways to fix our unbroken brain.

Work with our wiring instead of against it.

RESOURCE
Lack of information or need of a tool

Building on the "Progress" domain, I wanted to give us some reminders about how to reach for resources more quickly. And of course, we won't just be getting the writing advice. I will also be talking about why each of these resources might be helpful and who can benefit from them.

Obviously, I am not a person who believes all resources are equally applicable to everyone. And there are definitely patterns to why certain resources work and others don't, for everyone individual person. When we go through these cards, in the Resource domain, I will attempt to explain why certain things work and others don't.

Here's hoping this will be helpful in choosing which tools to use. Each resource fixes a specific problem. My goal here will be to address the problem in addition to the *why* it works.

And more specifically, what problems it will **not** fix. That's just as important.

. . .

SURPRISE
Getting bored or losing interest

THERE'S A REASON I DECIDED TO TACKLE THIS one last. Because it's alphabetically last. (Haha!) Also, when we are wired to need to be interested in our books, we've always heard the rhetoric about "If it bores you, it will bore the reader."

That's just not the case for many of us. Many writers have a higher threshold of need for new-and-different than any reader will ever have. We get bored easily, and that can cause a lack of progress in the novel or screenplay or piece of writing.

The goal of this domain is to provide some impetus for you to surprise yourself. Often, when new-and-different-needing writers try to write predictably (or even to-market), they get stuck more easily. If you're committed to doing that (writing intentionally to structure or writing intentionally to trope or exception), then you'll likely need the surprise elements more.

Also, I'm just going to throw out there: it's possible to write a story with structure without intending the structure to be there. But that's another topic for another time.

This domain is a little different in that I often encourage writers to go here, to surprise themselves, even if they don't have a high need for new-and-different, just because breaking out of fixed thinking can sometimes show us what the real problem is.

I had a client once who kept getting stuck at a certain point in her book and a highly creative friend of mine said, "What if you just skipped ten years ahead between these chapters?" Surprise.

Of course, the glitch was immediate, and the pushback was, "But in the genre expectations…"

My friend said, "Right, but what if you ignore the genre expectations?"

"I can't."

"As a thought experiment, then? What would happen if the character was ten years older?"

The lightbulb came on.

"I'm starting the story in the wrong place."

The fixed commitment to the story they thought they had to tell was causing them to miss the actual source of the stuck-ness. The story itself wasn't beginning early enough, and that would change everything.

It's important to note, they didn't skip ten years ahead when they wrote the manuscript. That was just the surprise thinking they needed to change their perspective.

We often resist thinking outside convention or norm because we're afraid of going off-track or we're afraid of doing something that will make the readers frustrated. But when nothing else is working, even for people who don't need the new-and-different, surprise can often be the thing that reveals the progress of the story.

Even if you have to create a separate document to progress in the surprise way in case you need to trash it... I will often suggest doing some of these Surprise actions, just as a way to break out of the thinking that's causing the problem.

AND THERE WE HAVE THE SIX DOMAINS. NOW, let's jump into the tool itself. First, the workbook exercises to diagnose the stuck. Then, the fixes themselves and their whys.

FOUR

Using This Book

IF YOU'RE GOING TO USE THE TOOL immediately, you can skip to Step Seven. But if you want to create the master Stuck List, follow this process.[1]

STEP ONE

Get out a pen and paper. Don't do this on your computer. Hand write this (even if you hand write on your tablet program).

STEP TWO

Make or print a list of your last (up to 15) books. If you're able, grab a calendar, as well, just in case you need it.

STEP THREE

Find a quiet place. It might be your car, parked in the garage (turned off, of course), or it might be in your kitchen. But find a place where you have some space and quiet to think.

Set aside half an hour or longer to really dig into this work. We want you to do as thorough a job as you can.

STEP FOUR

Think of the last times you were stuck in your manuscript. Where were they? (List each book, and where the stuck-ness happened.)

STEP FIVE

What eventually un-stuck you in each of those books? (Even if it was "the answer just came to me.")

STEP SIX

Look for common patterns. If you went back and re-read the book in five instances, note that. If you binge-watched a show (different or same), if you took a day off, if you did anything "the same", note that here.

Were there big-picture patterns? Do you have to distract yourself? Do you have to take time off? Wait for the deadline pressure to get real? What is the big-picture pattern?

STEP SEVEN

Go through the six domains of the cards and read the diagnostic at the beginning, then read through each card.

STEP EIGHT

Pull the cards that resonate the most. Put them in order of how much they resonate (or how often you typically use them).

STEP NINE

Keep that list of actions near you so you can get regularly unstuck without having to do in-the-moment diagnostics.

STEP TEN

Pull the card. Do the action on the card. (Or if you're not using the physical deck, write those pieces of advice in order on your piece of paper and keep that paper near you.) The goal is to refer back to the prioritized list as often as possible when you are stuck, just as a reminder of how to get yourself unstuck.

IF YOU WANT TO PULL RANDOMLY

I imagine some of you will use the Stuck List advice similarly to a tarot deck, where you pull a card at random. Also totally fine with that. I tried to collect as comprehensive a set of advice as I could, given the breadth of coaching experience.

REPETITION IN THE BOOK

I apologize ahead of time if I repeat some phrases a lot, or if I repeat an explanation in a couple of places. Because I had to make this book usable by "poking around," in addition to by reading from front to back, I had to make some editorial decisions about repeated sentences (where you might see the same sentence in two or three chapters). I apologize ahead of time if you are reading this from start to finish. I needed to make this fully usable for people who were going to utilize it as a companion to the deck, as well as to people who weren't going to use the deck at all. Thank you for your patience with that.

IF THERE'S SOMETHING MISSING

If you always use a piece of advice that I didn't directly give, please add it to your stuck list. You can also visit our Better-Faster Academy page on Facebook where we have regular free public coaching sessions. We almost always have questions submitted about getting stuck, as it's something writers regularly experience. You can always join one of our monthly public live coaching sessions if you want more direction or have questions.

But again, the goal of the deck is to be self-sufficient.

If you end up getting the deck, we made some blank cards specifically for you to write your own advice. No tool anyone ever makes will be 100% comprehensive for every person, although I tried my best with this one. Just know, this tool is made for you to customize. So if you need further customization, please make it work for you, but do reach out to ask us if you have questions.

Part II
First Domain: Clarity

If you need the Clarity cards, you'll often hear yourself asking the following questions:

What should happen next?

What would they do here?

Why can't I make them X?

Where would they go from here?

Who even are these people?

As we mentioned earlier, Clarity is often about blurriness or fuzziness in the upcoming parts of the book.

Let's get into the most effective Clarity advice. Just know, of course, not all of these will work every time.

Pay attention to your intuition and to the *why* behind why each piece of advice works.

Clarity 1

Get out a journal and hand-write about why you can't make progress in this work.

ADDITIONAL DOMAIN: Progress

Journaling is a tactic often encouraged by a vast number of writing teachers, but I want to talk a bit about *why* journaling works to promote clarity.

Not every person processes information in the same way or at the same speed. When you have a high need for clarity, your processing is almost always more voracious. Sometimes, that means you need to think more or process more in order to give more clarity.

Typing is often faster than our internal processing can work. Talking is definitely faster. But hand writing can be a bit slower and offer more of a chance for clarity to process at the same speed as our thought.

When I organized these pieces of advice into the categories, I was looking for the overlap between why the advice works and what problem it solves. Hand writing helps to slow down the output to a level of speed conducive to clarity. And it works because clarity progresses in layers. We understand, then we understand more, then we understand more. We do not generally reach complete clarity in a moment. It is layered over time.

Hand writing allows for that layering to happen without needing to talk (which is often faster than clarity can present), but also without sublimating the clarity into a place it won't be accessible.

Not all of you need this explanation, of course, but here's what I suggest if you tend to get stuck because you're not sure what happens next.

Get out a piece of paper and write the following prompts:

Here's what I know about the story so far.

Here's what I don't know about the story.

Here's why I feel stuck.

If one sticks out as the one you want to follow, by all means, go for it. But if you're not sure which to pick, start with the first one. When clarity is the thing we need, the biggest frustration is that we often don't know what we have to do to progress. But if we can be clear about what we already know, we can often free write our way into the story reappearing.

If you get to the second and third prompts, where the "I don't know" is bigger, then the free writing will become more important. Sometimes clarity of thought has to come at the sacrifice of emotions and that's often what free writing brings up.

The most common responses to the second and third prompts are, "I'm frustrated that I can't make progress." And that's rational. It's frustrating when our brains don't offer their clarity on command. But our brains are not doing this intentionally. They don't keep answers hidden because they are sabotaging us or because we secretly hate ourselves. No. Our brains are just all wired differently.

So sometimes, we really need to express our frustration the same way we would express a wound. So often, the things we need to do become apparent after we express the frustration.

Let me give you a few examples I commonly see:

"This book should be going faster. I don't know why it isn't. I've been going slow ever since that scene where the main character found her father's journal..." And then it'll devolve into a discussion about the plot that might actually be productive.

"I have no idea what's supposed to happen next. I have them at the door and I need to get them to the office. But I'm not sure who's between the door and the office.

I need to figure this out." And then you've uncovered the thing you don't know (which is what you need to discover in order to find clarity about the next steps).

"I'm mad that I can't make progress. It's the holidays and I never have time." And then it'll devolve into all the reasons why you're not making progress. Almost always, we're outlining exactly why we're not making progress when we're expressing our emotions. We just don't see it (or we don't think the reasons are valid). But sometimes we do actually need to see it all laid out on the page so we'll acknowledge when life is keeping us from writing.

We may not like the reasons. But we will almost always find clarity about the reasons when we do this live journaling.

If the reason is a reason, it usually meets the criteria of having been out of your control. If the reason is an excuse, it almost always has some level of control. I do not have control over whether or not it's the holidays (or my kids are out of school, etc.). I do have control over whether or not I open the internet first.

But.

"I don't write because I open Facebook" is both a reason and an excuse. I have some control over whether or not I open Facebook. Although if you just thought, "I want to open Facebook now," you are addicted and you need to aggressively not open Facebook.

You've crossed over into "not in control" land when you are addicted, and then the only problem becomes when you know you're addicted, but you gratify the urge anyway.

When a little addicted part of you says, "I can open Facebook really quick," and you believe it, even though every single day of your life when you've "really quick" opened TikTok or Instagram or Facebook or email or your ads dashboard, you have lost hours to it... why are we still believing this addicted part that's telling us "really quick" like it doesn't know better.

Really Quick Is A Lie.

The part that has the control and does not exercise the control is the part we want to change. But I cannot know I'm addicted to Facebook, then open it, and also be angry with myself for staying on Facebook so long. What do you expect, Willamena? You're addicted. You have no control.

Sometimes, what you see as excuses for not moving faster are really just reasons, and you need to accept that what happened happened, decide what to do differently, and move on. But sometimes, you need to process in order to find clarity about what's really going on.

The goal at the end of these journal sessions is the identification of what's keeping me from making progress. If you have the answer, you know what you need to do. If you don't yet have your answer, you may need to pull another card.

PROGRESS DOMAIN: Often, we find that writing about writing will turn into writing part of the manuscript, so the "next step" if I'm not sure what to do might be "write about writing" just to get the wheels greased to get words flowing.

Clarity 2

Read the last chapter or the last 2000 words you've just written.

ADDITIONAL DOMAIN: Progress

A lot of advice for authors warns against going back and re-reading what you've written. (And I know a lot of us feel like "going back" is the antithesis of "moving forward." But that's just not true.)

When going back over the last chapter helps to produce clarity, it happens because of three major causes.

1. You've forgotten a detail that you need in order to progress. Often, when we write, we sublimate certain details (like the direction someone left a house or the throw-away emotional comment the villain made in that last scene). When we've forgotten a clue we left for ourselves, we must reacquaint. No amount of thinking is going to substitute for re-contextualizing. If

this regularly happens to you, no worries—it's normal. You need that detail.

2. You've lost one of the thru-line threads. We don't only sublimate details. Sometimes we sublimate motivations and emotions, and we need to re-read them to remember them. In fact, a good portion of the "cycle" drafting I see is writers going back to pick up the threads they dropped without realizing it. There's no tool that will fix this (no matter how logical it might seem to try remembering to write down threads in a journal or on a spreadsheet). Going backwards is the best solution.

3. You need to re-immerse in order to find clarity. Sometimes, the going backwards is less about a specific detail or plot motivation, and it's more about being "inside the wardrobe." If I need to be inside the wardrobe in order to write the book, and I've fallen out of the world's context, re-reading can often solve this problem.

Solving one of these problems would mean that you'd gain clarity, which is, again, the point of this domain. To be more clear about how to progress.

You can usually tell when you need to do this because you'll have an instinct to go back. (And of course, most of us try to talk ourselves out of this instinct because we've been taught that only words-on-the-page-equals-forward-progress.)

Of course, you can random-draw this card anytime you'd like. But when it belongs on your Stuck List, you'll see a history for yourself in needing to go back.

(And also, the 2000 words was just a placeholder. It might be one chapter. It might be two or three. But start with one, or with 2000 words if your chapters are quite long. Just as a for instance, my average mystery chapter is 3000 words and four scenes long. I never need to go back more than about 2 scenes. But I've learned this about myself by experimentation. If this happens to you regularly, experiment with how far back you need to go so you can get a sense for the predictability.)

PROGRESS DOMAIN: WHEN WE LABOR UNDER the assumption that only words on the page cause us to move forward, we lose the very important reality that each of those miles (from the Progress Domain explanation in Chapter 3) has to be driven in order.

In this way, re-reading previous words is moving forward because the next mile that needs to be driven is the mile of "re-contextualizing" yourself in what you've written.

If you are the kind of person who needs to go backward in order to make forward progress, it's so much easier and faster to accept this and to go backwards as quickly as you can.

You can still maintain the worry that you'll get stuck back there (that worry might keep you from getting stuck in the revision), but if you have to go backward, you will eventually have to go back.

Might as well go sooner rather than later.

Clarity 3

Too many characters, Stacy. Put some back.
(This is the obligatory "do you have too many people to keep track of?" card. Even just asking the question... is everyone absolutely necessary? What would happen if you took one of them completely out of the story?)

ADDITIONAL DOMAIN: SURPRISE

There are some "complexity-friendly" personality traits that make us more likely to proliferate characters. Of course, some writers make a bedrock style out of overloading us with characters. But many writers prefer only to use a smaller number to keep them easily memorable for readers. If you regularly find yourself with unnecessary characters, it's always a good idea to ask the question, "do you have too many people" especially in an individual scene.

Sometimes, the overwhelm of too many motivations can cause stuck-ness, but not present itself easily. In fact, whenever I coach a writer who's feeling overwhelmed by how much is going on, I almost always ask them this question.

The other question we regularly ask is, "What would happen if you took out this character?" And then repeat that question over and over about multiple different characters. If everyone is necessary, then they're necessary. But sometimes, just asking the question can help you process over the character's purpose in the scene enough that you can decide if you need them or not.

The ability to see someone's usefulness (or uselessness) in a scene is often tied to thinking about the scene with a perspective of a bird's eye. It's harder to get to that bird's eye view when you're immersed in the scene.

It's also possible that you feel like you have to have too many characters because they all came together. (Like a raiding party all showed up in the same place.) But you haven't asked questions like, "Do they all need to be 'on camera' at the same time?" In fact, isolating characters into pockets might be enough of a difference maker. You might not actually have to kill any characters off at this point.

I mean, we'll get to that later...

SURPRISE DOMAIN: When we use this for the surprise domain, we actually ask people to take one character out. To rewrite the scene without at least one of the characters. See what happens.

That element of "guess what, you have to think about this scene differently than you had" can often bring some clarity to a situation that was blurry in the past. It can reveal motivations and actions that weren't previously known.

Clarity 4

Close your eyes and imagine the 360 view your character is seeing right now. What would they interact with in their immediate environment?

So OFTEN, WE WRITE WITHOUT A CLEAR SENSE of where we are and how that environment might impact a person.

When you're imagining the 360 view, it might help to go somewhere that reminds you of the place. It might be helpful to stand in the middle of a crowded bakery, to see what you notice. Or to put yourself into a forest. Smell, listen, feel.

The bugs, the wind, the sweet sagebrush. Aaaahhhh.

Would something in the environment be in the way? Would it be hot there? Cold? Is there a monument near them? Are there people? What are all the people doing there?

If you are a sense-of-place writer, you're likely to need more data about the environment than if you aren't. In fact, many people who write by sense-of-place would benefit from physically being in a location that reminds them of where they're writing about.

Of course, if you do a dialogue-only draft, or if you have to add all the scenery and setting on a different draft, this isn't going to work for you. But that's ok, too. Not everything should work for everyone. Just know it's ok to pass on this one if you don't tend to be aware of the environment of your characters or scenes.

Not everyone needs to.

Clarity 5

Who is in the scene with your POV character right now? How do they feel about that person?

ADDITIONAL DOMAIN: EMOTION

When you're writing about multiple characters in a scene (and especially if you're deep into the POV of the main character), it's common for the other characters' emotions to get buried a bit. But when it's necessary for the other characters to change the trajectory of a scene, you might get stalled out because they're not doing the work they need to do to stop or change your POV character.

If you're writing more than one character, consider pausing to label the emotions the other person is (or people are) feeling. What kind of action would that produce in them?

Of course, not everyone is aware of the emotions of the characters, so if this doesn't resonate with you, feel free to skip. But for those of us who swim in motivations and emotions of our characters (consciously or subconsciously), clarifying how the surrounding people feel can be really helpful.

And then take it a step beyond. It isn't just "what's the emotion" but it's also "what actions would that emotion produce?" Emotions are always productive. They should produce some kind of action.

EMOTION DOMAIN: IF YOU'VE NEVER USED AN emotion wheel before, I would recommend checking out that tool. Sometimes, having the right words to put to the emotions that are swirling around in the story can be really helpful. Clarity about emotion is one of the bedrocks of emotion-forward writers. (Even if you don't think about it when you write, or you don't name a lot of emotions as you write, knowing what the contextual emotions are can really help.)

Are they sad? Disappointed? Frustrated? Hiding? Repressed? (This is why I love the emotion wheel so much.) There's so much range to all the different labels.

Clarity 6

What does your character want right now? In this next scene? Can you give them something to want? Or skip to a place where they want something?

ADDITIONAL DOMAIN: Progress

While there are a lot of tools in the world to help figure out the bigger picture "wants" or "goals" of a character, I think we sometimes get too caught up in trying to get those things right, we miss the opportunity of desire to move us forward.

If you've ever read *Reclaim Your Author Career* by Claire Taylor, you'll be familiar with the idea of the Enneagram as a motivation in our author careers. Claire uses the idea of core fears and core desires as motivators for how we make decisions as business owners and authors. Every decision an author makes can be traced to some desire they have (in the moment, or as a big, driving force).

Sometimes, we get so caught up in finding the big, driving force for our characters, we miss the fact that they have desires in an individual scene. Are they trying to find something? Do they need to talk to someone? What are they hoping will happen when they meet that person? What will happen when they find the thing?

They're driven by some kind of desire.

It may be a big-picture motivation (like the way Enneagram core desires can have an overriding theme in our lives), or it might be a singular, momentary action.

The reason I differentiate between these two is, contrary to popular opinion, knowing the big-picture motivation of a character doesn't help every writer make forward progress.

I might know that my character's story goal is "to find her father and kill him." That's a pretty big goal and it sounds like there's a lot of motivation under that goal. But it might not help me to know that goal when I'm stuck with a lack of clarity about what she should do when she meets her love interest.

(Those of you who are wired for those big-picture goals to make individual decisions easy are thinking, "But no, Becca, that's easy… when she meets her love interest, she's so consumed by her desire to find her father that she ignores them." Right, Jason, I get that you can make that connection easily. But not everyone can.)

When you're naturally wired to look at big, over-arching goals as a way of determining scene-level actions, then just the initial question, "what does your character want" will produce an immediate clarity for you about what should happen next.

But for others, we need a little more granular prodding. (And even still, thinking about motivations, desires, hopes, etc, isn't going to help some of us. So if this isn't for you, skip this card. Or take this advice out of your rotation.)

The granular prodding might be as easy as asking what they're hoping to accomplish in this scene. Or if they aren't hoping to accomplish something, then can you give them something to accomplish? What's keeping them from getting the thing they're hoping to get?

And then we get to the PROGRESS part of this advice.

PROGRESS DOMAIN: SOMETIMES, A character not wanting something is a signal that you should skip to another place in the manuscript where they do want something. Not skip to start writing there, but cut everything that doesn't involve them wanting something. This kind of advice isn't for everyone. Of course. But sometimes, we need the reminder.

We'll talk a little more about skipping later, and what kind of benefit that produces. But when we're stuck, I think it's always worth at least asking the question if this is a part we need to write. Does this belong on page, or can we skip it? Even just asking the question can bring clarity.

Clarity 7

When was the last time your plot changed trajectory? Is there any tension on the page you're currently writing? Do you need to change direction?

ONE OF MY SCREENWRITING PROFS DESCRIBED plots as a roller coaster and told us to think about trajectory in our writing the way roller coaster designers think about how to structure a ride.

"You always want the trajectory to change direction," he said. "They get used to the story going down, then it goes up. They get used to it going up, then it goes down."

That metaphor sort of blew my mind when I first heard it, because in learning to write novels, I'd always thought of the three act structure (or five acts, if you're writing mystery). But this new metaphor helped me immensely in my novel writing, in addition to whatever script I was working on.

I'm not suggesting every scene should switch trajectory. (Although some of you who write higher action genres might have that level of roller-coaster-ing.) But this advice is more meant for people who struggle with the saggy middles. And this is advice I often give when I see someone stuck in the 40%-60% range of their book.

How long has it been since your narrative changed direction? Since the protagonist didn't get what they wanted? Since they were presented with a challenge?

Even if you don't change direction at the end of every scene, I think it's still beneficial to have this card around for asking the question to bring clarity.

Has there been too much "give them what they want" or "make them happy" or "don't challenge them" recently? Are they headed primarily in one direction and nothing is getting in their way?

(And again, always caveat with, if you write in a genre where there aren't major roller coasters, then maybe your trajectory only needs to change a few times. But if it's been too long, then there will definitely be a drag, and that can stop our progress.)

There's a class in the Margie Lawson Academy where she uses markers (or highlight colors) to track certain things throughout the manuscript. One of the most valuable tools I ever learned was how to track tension, and Margie is a master at teaching that. The class itself may not get you unstuck, because it's an editing class, but having that tool in your tool belt might be really helpful.[1]

When was the last sentence of tension I wrote? Do I see tension on the page?

Even just asking the question can help to provide clarity about what's coming next. Again, in the clarity section, we're looking for things we can do to make the blurry forward motion a little more clear.

When you have any level of capacity to anticipate character actions by their emotion or motivation, asking questions about those emotions or motivations should at least help you decide if there's something missing.

That's often what this particular question helps to solve. Is there tension missing that I could be adding? And if you do need to change direction, but you can't think of anything to do to change that direction, there are some suggestions in the Surprise Domain later on. This might also be a place to go looking for help here.

Clarity 8

Is there someone off-stage (or off-camera) who wants something contrary to your current POV character? What are they thinking or doing?

I KNOW USING WORDS LIKE "STAGE" AND "camera" are very non-novel-y, so I apologize about that. Not everyone sees their story as a movie in their head they're transcribing. But I wasn't sure how else to describe this. So. Let's assume you don't have to see the story like a movie in order for this to work.

The reason I ask this question for clarity is because we spend so much time in the POV characters' heads, and we can sometimes forget that they aren't the only drivers of trajectory. (In fact, asking this question can sometimes help provide clarity for Card 7 in this domain, because we know there hasn't been a change in trajectory, but we're not sure how to create it.)

I took a class early in my career called the W-Plot by Karen Docter, and she has this method where she creates arcs (shaped like Ws) for each of the major characters. The protagonists have a W-shaped plot (where they start off high and end up high) and the antagonists have an M-shaped plot (where they start off low and end up losing).

Essentially, the high points on the antagonist's arc create the low points in the protagonist's arc. Just that whole concept blew my mind because it introduced the thinking-in-two-minds capacity into my writing. When I have an antagonist in my story, their motivations create problems for my protagonist.

Because I write murder mysteries, that physical trajectory is really easy to see. When the killer drops the body (they win at their goal of murder, even if it wasn't premeditated), that's the low point for the sleuth. And as the sleuth works to right that wrong, the murderer starts losing.

But they are deeply motivated to keep the murder a secret, so every time the sleuth has a win, the murderer loses and wants to win again. (Especially in cozy, these murderers are often trying to maintain normalcy for themselves, so they can be fairly aggressive in their desire to keep things from the sleuth.)

That's what creates the trajectory of a mystery. The desire of the murderer to keep the murder secret. If the murderer doesn't have any motivation to keep the murder secret... it's just not as interesting because the trajectory of the story can only last until the sleuth overcomes just not knowing things.

Anyway, I digress. But this idea of an off-stage person having a motivation is something that we don't ask when we're naturally stuck. We often get so focused on the POV character, when we need to focus more on what the antagonist would be doing (or, honestly, anyone else in the story who isn't the main character).

Even a friendly person can act as an antagonist at times.

In a romance novel, the best friend might be the person who signs the character up for a dating app. In that moment, the goal of the protagonist is to not date. That goal is antagonized when their friend signs them up for the service.

The motivations of non-POV characters can sometimes provide exactly the clarity we need in order to make more progress. In fact, I see a lot of saggy middle issues that stem from not having any opposition to the POV character's goals or motivations. No one outside of the POV character wants anything. And the clarity that comes from "what would the best friend do if their goal was to get their friend to date" can be really helpful.

In fact, I would venture to say, a lot of slower-moving plots suffer from there being nothing opposing the POV character other than their own internal conflict. If no one in the book wants anything the POV character doesn't want... that might be a problem.

(I'm tempted to say, definitively, it would be a problem. But I just know there's a Joe out there who can give one example of one great book where that doesn't happen. So I'll caveat with… at least think about asking the question.)

Just ask the question about other people's desires or motivations. See if anyone around them wants anything contrary to what they want. Or if there is an actual villain, sometimes it does help to track the villain's movements, to help with the trajectory of the story. Just to know what they would have been doing to oppose the protagonist can sometimes provide the clarity we need.

Clarity 9

What matters to your character right now? What can they not stand to lose? What would they do to protect that?

THIS IS A DIFFERENT QUESTION ABOUT THE clarity of direction, but not completely unrelated to the "what do they want" question. Specifically, this is about the last question. "What would they do to protect" the thing they can't stand to lose.

If you're not able to connect with what the character wants, it might be partly that the motivation doesn't run deep enough. But if you think of the thing a person can't stand to lose, that's often easier to visualize or to understand.

When you think of taking away the thing they can't stand to lose, that can also create a cascade of emotions, as well. In fact, because it's common for writers who are emotion-responsive to not want to put their characters through pain, it's possible to be blocked only because your characters are potentially going through pain.

This question is meant to check in on whether or not the characters' desires are in any danger. If they aren't in danger at all, that can be a bad sign, as well.

Once again, I'll say, I'm not trying to make a case for the fact that every story should have life-and-death stakes. But if there's nothing they're afraid to lose... I just wonder if it's worth asking if we're digging enough.

Or if we might be trying to protect the characters from having to go through the worst thing for them.

I know, I know. Just asking the question.

Clarity 10

Do you know what your POV character was like at the age of:
Five?
Ten?
Fifteen?
Twenty?

TW: Skip this chapter if you have triggers for childhood trauma.

Not everyone can know their characters before they write. Sometimes, even when you think you know them (you do a bunch of character work ahead of time), you don't really know them until you get into the book.

When writers are more wired to discover their characters through the book (even when they might outline, but the outline will get malleable the farther they get into the text), they often get stalled out by a lack of clarity about who the character *really* is.

And by "really," I mean, the character you've written, and not the character you thought you created. Almost always, when writers are wired for character discovery, they *get to know* the characters as the book progresses. This might change details about the story that seemed solidified, but which become more fluid after time, as other details are added or discovered.

(If you're not a person who discovers character along the way, you can ignore this one, because you might not need this question as much.)

The reason I went backward, to the ages I did, was because the changes in the character (especially ones that impact story trajectory) are often about what's really motivating them or (if you're using Michael Hague's Inner/Outer Journey) what's their real wound.

These ages are the more formative ages for the wounds we actually receive. I'm not as worried about the specific ages as I am about the age ranges. Each of the different ages represents a different type of formative wound that characters will act out, heal, or learn to integrate (depending on their place in the story).

FIVE: This represents anything that happened to them before they would really remember it. Often, this is something like having lost a parent they never knew, or a sibling being taken from them, or something that would leave a large imprint, but which might not come up in conversation the first few times you'd talk to a person.

TEN: This represents anything that happened to them in formative years that was traumatic. Typically, this is ages 8-12 in stages of development, and is the most common seat for trauma repetition. (Again, excepting things like sexual violence and physical violence, which can have a trauma impact at any age.)

FIFTEEN: This represents older adolescence. These are often either romantic wounds (the first crush, the first romantic partner) or not-a-kid-anymore wounds.

TWENTY: This represents the "first launch" wounds. Things that might have happened to your character when their adulthood was still just forming. Young adulthood and college age. And this might be more the territory of motivation acquisition (like "when I decided to become a doctor" or "when I got married" or things of that nature).

Again, these aren't meant to be prescriptive. But the questions are meant to bring more clarity about the things you don't yet know about the character.

So often, when I coach writers who are character-discoverers, they reach a point in the manuscript (and it's often after the midpoint) where they discover something about the character's past that changes things about the first 60% of the book. And when that happens, I often see them struggling to go back and realign the manuscript. Instead, they look for tools to fix this, and try to know more and more about the character.

But if you're wired this way, things you discover about the character are more real than things you invent about the character. So at some point in the book, you're going to have to go back to something that formed them. This is exactly like real relationships with real people. They don't tell you their childhood trauma when you first meet them (unless you are their therapist or counselor).

If you are stuck at around 55-70% and you're writing character driven fiction, just consider doing this exploration. The clarity about who they used to be might help.

Clarity 11

Open the manuscript and ask, "Can I write the next sentence?" If you can write the next sentence, write it. If you can't, pull another card or go think about what will happen next until you can see it. Thinking is working.

ADDITIONAL DOMAIN: PROGRESS

If you are wired to be a thinker, it is likely that you will hit multiple points in your novel where you need to stop and think about what happens next. This isn't a deficiency. We shouldn't be trying not to think... and I really do understand the frustration.

I am also wired this way.

But thinking isn't evil. And it isn't the opposite of writing. Thinking produces writing. So if we could just think more effectively or efficiently, we could get the best of both worlds.

The biggest issue with being wired to think is often the inertia. I stop to think about what's supposed to happen in the book and I don't start moving forward again.

This tool solves the problem of inertia without any of the damaging "just stop thinking" rhetoric.

And by the way, when I say, "Thinking is working," I also mean the kind of thinking we do when we can't focus our thoughts only on the thing we're supposed to be focused on. When we start thinking and our mind wanders. When we start thinking and we remember to pay the bills.

Not all thinking has to be conscious.

But if you're wired to think about things until you reach clarity, no surprise the book will also require that thinking. And if you leave the manuscript and you find yourself thinking about other things, and you lose that day to the other things, then the next morning, do the "can I write the next sentence" thing.

The goal of asking this question is to focus our minds on "what is clear" and "what is not clear." If I pause in the manuscript because there's something ahead that feels fuzzy, but the thing I'm focused on is farther ahead than the next sentence, I don't necessarily need to think about that thing yet. Plus, writing the next sentence might help me get clarity about the thing I still need to think about.

The key is, you're wired to think, but that doesn't mean you can't still ask the question about progress. I'd rather see us attempt progress each time we have a bout of thinking, rather than wait completely for clarity.

(Also, you may do things that don't look like progress in the search for clarity about what's happening next in the manuscript. You might, gasp, procrastinate as a way of trying to let your brain take a break from what you're writing or working on. This can still be progress, but we'll handle that in the Progress domain.)

If you keep opening the manuscript and asking, "can I write the next sentence," then you're at least working against the inertia. That's all we want. Embrace the thinking, but work against the inertia.

And the answer might be, "No, I can't," and that won't be a failure. It will be a wild success because at least we've done the work we can do for the time being.

If the answer is no, I would also consider pulling another Clarity card. Just in case there's additional clarity that would help the forward motion.

So often, when we're wired for needing to think to find clarity, we need to make sure we're always opening the manuscript just to keep the fear of the manuscript at bay. The more comfortable we can get with, "I want to make progress, and thinking can be progress," the easier it will be to embrace the thinking.

It's amazing how often our intuition about what we need to do next is actually right. Hopefully, the experience of reading this book can help us to trust intuition more often.

Clarity 12

What trope is your story following? (I know, Steve, I know, you're so unique, but there's a trope of some kind in every story...)

TROPES ARE AN INTERESTING TOPIC TO BRING up among writers. In fact, I've seen fights break out at writer's conferences over whether or not tropes are a good thing. (No punches were thrown, but it was close.)

I feel like we get caught up in this discussion for personality reasons and we don't realize it. So I want to disconnect any expectation of preference from this discussion.

It doesn't matter if you like tropes or not.

If your story resonates with an audience, it will have a trope in it somewhere. Even if you didn't intend to put it there. Even if you wanted to make it the newest, most different thing you could possibly make it.

Because tropes are simply repeated story structure. They are what makes story resonate with us. And many tropes are there unintentionally. Many writers do not intend to put tropes in their story. A trope is simply a resonant structure (because tropes are, inherently, structural).

What I mean is: a trope is how a reader makes sense of a story, even if they don't know this is what they're doing. When we see a fish out of water, we inherently want to see them get back into the water because we know they will die without oxygen.

Repeated structures create reader expectations. Fulfilling and subverting reader expectations is the joy and craft of writing.

But when you have a fish out of water who doesn't get back into the water (a person who starts off with the town as an adversary, and ends with the town as an adversary), you haven't really subverted the trope as much as you have just written a different trope.

The self-sufficient outcast.

So what started off as one trope expectation (closing the loop of the new-person-to-town by making them part-of-the-town) just becomes a different set of expectations (the new-person-in-town who doesn't get accepted by the town and instead forges their own way and becomes "better" than the town). This is just the difference between *The Shawshank Redemption* and *The Addams Family*.

A trope is an expectation promise that's opened at the beginning of a story and architecturally supported throughout the story, and then closed at the end. Tropes resonate with audiences because they are familiar. Some familiarity is good for audiences.

What won't happen is writing a story that resonates that doesn't have a trope in it. It's just not possible. Resonance is all about familiarity. About seeing something that structurally pleases us. (Even if the structure is post-modern. It's still structure.)

The reason I argue so heavily for tropes as architecture is because I see a significant amount of clarity-seeking that's actually about recognizing when I've opened a loop I need to close. When we've made a story promise that needs to get fulfilled. And instinctively, we know that structure is just sitting there, open, and needing to be closed.

IMPORTANT CAVEAT: If you are not aware of the tropes you're writing, you may have to process this with someone in order to get at it, and it'll be less about finding the trope, and more about finding the loop you opened that you need to close. What story promise did you instinctively make that you haven't yet wrapped up? What would make the character feel fulfilled? What would get rid of their uncertainty?

Some of us are more conscious of the tropes, and we are intentionally creating situations that have a solution. If you are this person, you might instinctively think about the trope or the story promise, or you might put multiple tropes and you need to make sure you go back through the story and find the loops you need to close.

Did you open a loop somewhere that needs closing?

Clarity 13

Take out a piece of paper and draw your current scene layout. Where are your characters? Where do they need to go? How will they get there?

ADDITIONAL DOMAIN: Progress

This might feel like a strange request, but when we have a high need for clarity, it's very common to get stopped by things that are hidden in our subconscious.

If you imagine the thinking you would normally do, as you're stuck in the manuscript, these clarity cards are meant to shortcut to something you would get to at some point in your thinking process anyway.

So often, when we aren't as "located" in the physical place of the story, something that creates a change in the physical environment can create pause. Where I see this happen a lot are in the following places:

- fight scenes
- scenes with more than two characters
- scenes with unknown environments (like a cave or something where you don't know the boundaries yet)
- love scenes
- black moments (crisis points)

Anything with choreography or physical exploration, basically. If you can block out the action, like you would if you were going to choreograph it for stage, it can make the clarity happen faster.

This stuck-ness will feel like overwhelm, most of the time. Like "I'm not sure what should happen next" or "I'm not sure where they should go." Just draw a 2-D representation of the physical location where they are currently walking/waiting/standing, and then start to walk yourself through the physical blocking of what needs to happen in the next scene.

PROGRESS DOMAIN:

Hopefully it will be obvious that things like drawing scene outlines and thinking count as progress. I know it's hard for some of us to internalize that, but if it's required in order to make the next part of the book happen, then it's required.

And I don't even wish there was a way to get rid of the need for this. The reason our brains need these tools is because they have a particular way of creating story that is different from other people. I think that's the best news in the world. Different brains mean different stories and different stories mean happy readers.

While my progress as a writer, through the manuscript, might not be the easiest, at least I know it's the best.

Part III
Second Domain: Emotion

Wouldn't it be great if emotions just didn't matter at all? I know some of you are thinking that. In fact, I wouldn't be at all surprised if some of you are wondering how it's possible for emotions to be part of being stuck at all.

Well, my friend... won't you be surprised.

Not all of these pieces of advice are about our own emotions as writers. Some of them are about other people, and about even the characters. And if you're not a person who generally thinks emotions are worth thinking about, feel free to skip these.

But my guess is, they might play a bigger role than you hope.

(And of course, everyone who's fluent in emotions is starting to roll their eyes at how much I'm caveating this one. Let's jump in.)

NOTE: If the very idea of emotions impacting your writing seems unlikely to you or foreign, or you get frustrated with people who are impacted by emotions, you need to skip this whole domain. Just go right past it. Nothing to see here. I'm warning you, it's only going to frustrate you.

Emotion 1

**What is your POV character feeling right now?
How would a person act who is feeling that way?**

EMOTIONS ARE PRODUCTIVE. WHEN A PERSON feels an emotion, an action brews inside them. It might be a need to reach out for comfort. It might be to set a boundary. Any number of things. But emotions are signals that something needs to happen.

When a character is feeling an emotion, that can be an easy indicator about what type of action they might be taking, or what they would do next. And often-times, if we are not immersed in the emotion of the scene, we can miss the action cues.

If you think of the four primary positive emotions (joy, gratitude, hope, security) and the four primary negative emotions (sadness, fear, guilt, and anger), on a continuum from left to right, where would your character land right now?

How would someone act when they are feeling joy?

How would someone act when they are feeling gratitude?

How would someone act when they are feeling hopeful?

How would someone act when they are feeling secure?

How would someone act when they are feeling anger?

How would someone act when they are feeling fear?

How would someone act when they are feeling sad?

How would someone act when they are feeling guilt?

If you can't do that theoretically, then ask someone who seems to be fluent in emotional vocabulary. If you know anyone who is a teacher, doctor, therapist, or who works in customer service (jobs that interact a lot with the public), ask them what they think.

Sometimes, when we're disconnected from the character emotions, it's a signal that there isn't anything happening, which is why I'm being so thorough here about pushing for these questions. If you've thought through their emotions and they're not feeling anything, then either something needs to happen to them right now to create action (flip to the "Surprise" section), or there's something going on you're not connecting with.

I would tend to edge toward the former, just because I see it happen often where writers can struggle to do things to their characters that are painful (often because, the more empathetic they are, the more they're going to have to feel those emotions themselves). So while I don't want to assume we're all taking it easy on our characters, I at least want to represent that point of view here.

Emotion 2

Have you checked in with your positive outlook?
Do you need an infusion of positive thinking?

CAVEAT: NOT EVERYONE IS A "POWER OF positive thinking" person and I don't think we have to be. But keeping an eye on the flow of positive energy vs. negative energy can be a really helpful exercise.

If you are wired to respond to positive thinking, chances are good that you're keeping yourself balanced here already. But I would still just ask the question.

How is your positive mental attitude?

Are things in the world around you getting critical? Is there too much downside? Too many complainers? Are you looking ahead and not finding anything to make you feel hopeful about the future? If you're answering yes to a lot of these questions… this is the right card for you.

Think about the people who help you to look on the bright side. Find someone who's brimming with positive energy, and let them remind you of all the things that might go right in the world.

Also, just a reminder, a lot of people who are wired to be receptive to the energy around them get impacted by too much negativity around them, even when they're not aware. That's why we suggest the check-in.

And if this isn't for you, feel free to skip this card.

If you find your positive energy regularly drained consider two things:

1. Quit being on social media first thing in the morning. Even if you don't write first thing. We are not wired for easy control when it comes to the digital distractions in our lives because our biology is being preyed upon (even if it's unintentionally—but, trust me, it's often intentionally) by the stimulation the digital world provides. The earlier in your day you get onto social media or open your email or anything on the internet, the more likely you are to return to it all day long. And we think we have control over this, but we don't. When we have the most control is when we *first* experience it in the morning. Hold out as long as you possibly can, even if it's painful.

2. Quit watching the news. No matter what news you watch. The news is meant to be checked, not watched, as a friend of mine says regularly. If you *watch* news, it's entertainment, not information. Checking the news is

enough to be "in the know" (and even then, I'd still prefer we check less often—when things happen, we will find out about them). Many of us are consuming the news the way we consume information, but the information never changes.

If you are reluctant to do either of these, I would do a quick check-in with yourself.

Is this an addiction talking? (The impact of dopamine on our brains can lead us to continue consuming things that are bad for us just because they give us the good chemicals when we get them.) If it's an addiction, there will be a lot of resistance.

But there's an easy way to test. Just try it. For a week. Try not opening social media or watching the news until 5pm. Just try it. For seven days. That feeling of fear or worry that's coming up is a little drug dealer in your head worrying that it won't be able to get the hit it needs. And yes, there will be some pain involved. But I just want you to **test** if it will help your feelings of negativity and hopelessness or anxiety or competitiveness.

If this is something you regularly struggle with, just try it.

You can report back and yell at me later.

Emotion 3

Are you expecting too much from yourself? Do you need to ask for help?

OK, I GUESS WE'RE GOING FOR THE JUGULAR here in this domain. Phew. I should have had my coffee earlier this morning.

(And if you are reading this, but you're one of the people I warned to skip this domain… why are you still reading? Skip.)

Since the goal of this project is to talk about all the ways we're stuck, I have to cover the "life" sources in addition to the manuscript sources.

I cannot count the number of times I've sat down to coach a writer who is stuck in their manuscript where the notes section for the call is full of all the pain points of their busy life. And then, invariably, at the end of the notes, they'll say something like, "I just want to know why I'm so stuck."

The smile I give in that moment is a pained smile, but still, it's a moment of recognition.

When life is a lot, and it's causing us not to be able to make progress in the manuscript, I completely understand that frustration of, "but I still want to make progress." And some of the things writers add in their notes are genuinely too much for anyone to be expected to bear. Still, we have this desire to continue to make progress.

And it's not only from a place of monetary or financial pressure. Often, writing is an escape for many of us. And when life's pain is too much, we want to be able to escape into the manuscript. But that's often not possible because life is just too much.

In order to be able to disconnect from life and connect to the writing, many of us need space. We need to be able to think and have time to connect with the characters, but we have such limited time to get into the WIP (work-in-progress), we can't fully shut down the thoughts about life, family, work, and the world.

This lack of space doesn't keep us from expecting that we should be able to shut everything down, though. And this is where I have to often give the hard truth to a client/student: if you don't have the space to get lost because life's troubles are too monumental, then maybe writing is not the thing to escape into right now.

We usually do try to see if we can create some of that space, of course, but that often comes at a price.

Can I pay for child care?

Can I pay for a cleaning service?

Can I pay for my spouse to stop working?

Can I pay for an assistant to watch all my inboxes?

Can I pay someone to run my ads?

Can I pay someone to do my marketing?

Notice the word "pay" in all those sentences? The barrier of cost is significant when it comes to creating space from life, for most of us. (And those of us who have an easier time creating space are often taxing others around us without realizing it. So the people who are wired to notice when they're taxing others are more reluctant to ask for help because we know everyone is dealing with a lot right now.)

If this is something you're struggling with (not being able to create space), I highly recommend you go read my other books (*Dear Writer, You Need to Quit* and *Dear Writer, You're Doing It Wrong*). I know, I know, on those titles. But almost all of us are just doing too much.

(And no, I don't want you to quit writing. Just quit other things.)

Or watch the YouTube channel for all the "Quit" and "QTP" episodes on there. So much of this emotional overwhelm we feel as writers is related to how much we're expecting of ourselves that just isn't realistic.

Additionally, of course, if you are able to get support (from friends or family, spouse or partner, parents or children), I recommend it. Even tiny shifts like making a daycare co-op where you trade your kids with another parent every other day so you can have some space and quiet in your home.

Not everyone will struggle with this, obviously, so feel free to ignore the advice. But because I see this a *lot* in my coaching practice, I had to bring it up for general consumption when it's one of the reasons I so consistently see writers not writing.

Life is a lot. Adulting is a lot. You are not alone there. I feel this in my bones. And I hope this discussion was helpful, not painful. I know for some of us, it will be pain, because there is no option, but let me just end on this one positive note.

Nothing lasts forever. If you end up having to pause in your writing for a time because life is too much, know it will be there. Many of us have a lot of fear around having to take a break/pause from writing, and I completely get that fear. Know that it's your brain trying to help you, but it might not be the most helpful thing for you right now. It might be the best to take a break from writing while life is overwhelming. You can come back to it.

I know it sounds harsh to say "nothing lasts forever" and I'm not trying to minimize anyone's overwhelm. But when we come to books like this for help, my guess is, we already know subconsciously what we need to do, and we just need someone to remind us that it's okay to do what we know we need to do.

I hope this will be the last time I have a heavy conversation like this in the book—I hadn't intended to get this deep. But this is one area where I know, if you're having the problem this card suggests, you need to know it's possible to pause and resume.

Literally all the hugs right now.

Emotion 4

Are your characters in a black moment? Some writers get stuck when their characters are in rough places. Check in with your empathetic nature.

I HINTED AT THIS BEFORE, BUT WHEN WRITERS are highly empathetic, this is one of the things I see happen the most often. In fact, I can almost predict the characters are in a difficult emotional place, just by the way the writer talks about the book.

Avoidance.

When you are wired to easily have empathy for others, you are likely to have a deep emotional connection with your characters, even when you don't want to. That means, if your characters are going through a black moment, it's the same as if you had a friend sitting across from you at a coffee shop, going through the same experience, live and in person.

Emotions are not fictional. (In fact, that's why a lot of people read books at all, to feel the emotions vicariously.)

If you are in a place where you're avoiding going to the manuscript, and you are highly empathetic, try the following:

1. Start your day, early in the morning, with opening the manuscript first, and jump into the writing as quickly as you can. (If you need to prepare yourself first by walking or writing-about-writing, that's fine. But try to get into your manuscript before there are people around you, if you can.) Sometimes, the weight of others' emotions is too much to slough off when you're having to go to the black moment.

2. Leave the house. Go to a library or coffee shop (or, honestly, go park in your car somewhere that your family and friends can't find you) and get into a place where you won't be interrupted.

3. Clear the emotions. When you're finished writing the scene, do something to clear your emotions. Cry, take a shower, go for a walk or drive, punch a pillow, etc. Do something to express out the emotions so you don't hold them inside.

You might end up being emotionally impacted in a way that will affect how you interact with your family and friends after you write, so if this is the case, then try switching the morning writing to night writing. Just to see if that will help.

It might also be beneficial to regularly leave the house for longer time periods (like a writing retreat). When people are wired to be emotionally receptive, they often feel bad about oppressing other people with their emotions, so if it's more helpful not to be around people when you're highly emotional, find a way to escape the environment so you can safely enter and exit the black moment.

And then have a piece of chocolate. Or go for a run. Something to soothe that tension.

Emotion 5

Are you sick or tired? Do you need rest or space or care?

OH WOW, BECCA. YOU ARE JUST PUNCHING away in this domain, aren't you?

Because I spent some time talking about this in an adjacent way in Emotion 3, I won't belabor this again.

Let me just add:

Not wanting to be sick or tired is understandable. None of us want that. And when it's a source of frustration and pain for us, it's often something we don't want to talk much about.

But when we need rest, space, or care, that is what we need. Not wanting to need it won't help the need go away. Only fulfilling the need will help the need go away.

Expecting that we *shouldn't* have the need we have won't make the need go away. I wish it would.

And now, I'll stop talking about this. Promise.[1]

Emotion 6

Have you seen a character in a book or movie who feels similarly to your main character? What did they do?

ADDITIONAL DOMAIN: CLARITY

A lot of writers have a fear of watching movies or reading books in their genre, because they're afraid of copying. So I want to be careful to say here, I'm not saying if you don't go to a book or movie, you're doing it wrong.

I only mean, it's possible to look to other media for reference, and still not copy what they do or say. But some of us have an easier time of this than others.

If it helps to focus only on big-picture actions or big-picture emotions, rather than specific wording or dialogue, maybe talk through the scene with a friend instead of watching/reading it for yourself.

I have a writer friend I regularly do this with, where we break apart scenes in movies we've both seen to talk about how they fulfill tropes or how they emotionally lay out. We will often put the emotional arcs in terms of Strengths or Enneagram types to additionally help the arcs make sense and analyze what characters would do in that situation.

Anything that gives you an external reference, I think, is a good idea. Sometimes, seeing the emotions acted out by characters or real people can give us just the piece of data we need in order to understand what's really happening.

CLARITY DOMAIN: This was originally in the Clarity Domain, but I moved it into Emotion because it feels like it's more about the depth of the emotional arc than it is about intellectual clarity. But if you are the kind of person who doesn't feel emotions from other people, then intellectual clarity can happen with emotions as well. It just happens with analysis, rather than with internal vibe checks or emotions.

Both are valid.

Emotion 7

Are you in trauma? Or recovering from trauma? Would you benefit from therapy, coaching, or time off right now?

I FEEL LIKE I'VE COVERED A VERSION OF THIS in nearly every chapter in this domain, so I'm not going to re-hash anything I've already said. (Go read Emotion 3 and 5 for more on this topic.)

But there's a reason I have several different versions of this in the domain. Many of us are resistant to accepting the way that life impacts our writing, specifically because we see other people who are able to compartmentalize so effectively.

Let me say, for the record, someone else's ability to do something is of no relevance to you. Not that you can't look at how they are and want to be that way. (It's possible that what you need to do in your future self-development is to acquire skills that will aid in compartmentalization.)

But I often hear this phrase, "I don't know why they can do something I can't do."

You know why.

They're different from you. They have different brain wiring and different life experience. If you make rhetorical statements (statements that aren't meant to be responded to), or ask yourself rhetorical questions, that is the path to spinning out.

Never ask rhetorical questions. Always answer the question.

"Why can they write 1000 words in 30 minutes and I can only write 200?"

Because they have a differently-wired brain that allows them to do that. Are there skills you could add that would make you write faster than you write? Likely, yes. But that's not why you asked the question. You asked the question to feel the frustration.

"Why can they compartmentalize and I can't?"

Because they are wired differently and they acquired those skills in their life (likely before they were 28 years old, when our brain wiring has been more solidified—not unchangeable, but less changeable). Do you have the time to unwire the wiring you have? Do you have time and energy to acquire the skills they have? Do you have the natural abilities it will take to support those skills?

(And again, the answer might be, yes, you have the time and energy. And that's why I'm discussing this in the card where I talk about therapy or coaching. I highly recommend DBT/CBT/EBT[1] or EMDR[2] for skills work, and if you're really looking for long-term help, go to an Internal Family Systems specialist.)

I am not a therapist or a doctor. Coaches are not therapists or doctors. I'm a huge fan of therapy.

I don't even play one on TV.

When it comes to trauma responses and clinical skills acquisition, I don't think there's any substitute for seeing a great therapist.

I also want to make sure we aren't minimizing how hard it is to accomplish something like creativity (which takes so many different types of energy to accomplish) when our body is in fight or flight mode on a regular basis.

Emotion 8

_____

Do you like the book you're writing? I know, Courtney. I know. But at least ask the question.

THERE'S SOMETHING TO BE SAID FOR WORKING through a project even when you don't like it (especially when you're on deadline). And one of the Progress cards was originally going to be about that very thing.

But when you're the kind of person who does well just marching through things you don't like, you don't need my help with that one. You're already doing that.

Y'know who does need reminding?

People who are struggling so much with not liking what they're writing that it makes them not write.

And because there's so much rhetoric in the writing community about hating what you write, I think there's this sense of "this is my lot in life" and "I guess I'll just never like what I write" with some of us. So let me just ask the question.

What would happen if you stopped writing this book you don't want to write?

What if there's a reason why your dislike is stopping you? What if the reason is, this isn't the book for you to be writing? If you haven't ever considered that before, and it sounds foreign to you, skip to the next card.

But if this resonates, just think with me about this for a moment.

When we are wired to be fully engaged in what we're doing, and we have always been able to count on the like of something to guide us in the past, the lack of engagement is a sign. It might be a sign you shouldn't be doing the project you're doing.

No decision is final. Just allow yourself to think about it, for a second, without judgment. Maybe talk to a friend about it (one who won't judge you for asking the question).

If you're the kind of person who will never come back to a book once you leave it, then maybe this isn't the question for you. But if you know you have the capacity to come back to it, and your interest level is often a signal for you about whether or not to work on a project, then let yourself follow that signal.

Emotion 9

Alexis suggests: The American Lung Association used to have a slogan, "If you can't breathe nothing else matters." Sometimes, we get so wrapped up in everything going on around us, we forget to breathe - to pause and allow our brains (bodies) time to catch up or simply settle. So, breathe, my friend. The "3-2-4 Breath From Your Core" Technique not only rhymes but is a simple, easy to follow way to sneak in a quick pause in your day.

IN MY EARLY THIRTIES, I LOST A JOB BECAUSE I quit breathing. Some of you may have experienced this before. I was diagnosed with sleep apnea, and I finally had a reason for why I was perpetually behind and missing deadlines, falling asleep at work and never knowing it.

My coworkers would regularly come into my office and I would be sitting up at my desk, asleep. No one ever told me. To me, I was just blinking my eyes. That's how tired I was.

And it all stemmed from not breathing properly while I was sleeping. So when I saw this advice from Alexis, I got a visceral reaction to the words because I had such a specific experience.

To me, breathing is emotional because the lack of breath or the constriction of breath can cause so much pain.

When I first started watching TikTok, I ran across a creator who would regularly do a "breathe with me" video and every time it came on, I would watch at least twice because I could feel myself being constricted.

It wasn't until I'd been on TikTok for a year that I realized why that creator was so popular. So many of us are breathing in shallow, constricted ways because we are stressed and tired and the world is a lot. We're not getting full breath support, and we're not even realizing it.

So, my friend, do what Alexis suggests here.

Breathe in. Hold. Breathe out.

Just repeat that.

Breathe in. Hold. Breathe out.

And again.

Breathe in. Hold. Breathe out…

Emotion 10

Is someone around you in trauma? Do you need to tend to them before you can get some space for your manuscript?

WHEN SOMEONE ELSE'S TRAUMA IMPACTS US, it's often important to get the reminder that being wired to care about other people is a good way to be wired. Not being able to write when your friends or family need you is not a weakness. It's a strength.

And also, it can come from many Strengths in the CliftonStrengths© personality metric, as well.

So it isn't just a way to be wired, it's a way to be successful. That ability to be impacted by your relationships with others can be a huge asset when it comes to writing round and believable characters, or writing deep emotional arcs.

It just often also comes with the price of not being able to turn it off. Hopefully this domain has been helpful if you are wired this way.

And if you're not wired this way, maybe it will give you insight into your writer friends who are receptive, and how successful they are because of that amazing wiring.

In coaching writers, one of my goals is always to make no assumptions. Too often, when I'm first sitting down with someone, they're telling me all the things that are making them stuck, but they're assuming those can't possibly be the reasons why they're stuck.

It can't be that I'm moving across the country.

It can't be that I'm at home with my kids all day.

It can't be that I was just diagnosed with a major illness.

And I get why they have this feeling. Because those things, we can't change. I can't not be moving. I can't not have my children. I can't change a diagnosis. So if that's the reason, then I feel trapped.

But I'm here to tell you, ignoring a reason just because you don't want it to be the reason is never helpful. And it won't lead to getting unstuck. If you don't have the skills to compartmentalize (or if your trauma response manifests in blocking those skills), then we definitely have to deal with the hard truth of the environment.

Some of this domain is about that. About the things we wish we could explain away or ignore. And some of this domain is about how environment can often play a bigger role than we wish it would.

Tweaking circumstances can often help to produce progress, and whenever possible, we want to tweak. I promise, almost none of the advice is, "just accept that you won't be writing." Sometimes, of course, that is what we have to do. And we need to remind ourselves that we can always come back to it in another period of life, when stability has returned.

But my goal in this domain is to change what we can change and quit what we can quit to make the environment supportive of the writing.

Environment 1

Go for a walk. Listen to music or don't, but don't listen to podcasts or news. Let yourself think.

ADDITIONAL DOMAINS: Progress, Clarity

When I was a kid, one of the regular fantasies I had about being a writer was the idea of Charlotte Brontë wandering the Yorkshire moors in silence, listening to the wind and the whispers of story.

Even now, I'm off to Google how much it costs to move to Brontë Country. I still have that desire for isolation —specifically because my brain is wired to think until I reach clarity. Thinking is hard to do when people are talking to you and when you're expected to participate in things.

Many of us don't have a lot of alone time, and our writing suffers for it. When our brains need alone time, we should consider that "alone time" as a system requirement for optimal performance.

Something needed for the best story outcome.

So if you're a music person, by all means, let yourself have music on. May I suggest the Jane Eyre soundtrack. But my preference for this particular piece of advice is to try not listening to anything.

The desire to think and the desire to learn are not mutually exclusive, so it's possible to want to use the time alone to concentrate on the learning. But I want to put in a plug for shutting down the learning for some time and just giving your brain a chance to process.

We use a metaphor in our coaching when brains need a lot of thinking time, and that metaphor is train tracks.

There are only so many tracks in our brains that thought trains can take. Let's just say there are seven tracks. But thought trains might proliferate two and three times more than the tracks available.

Every train's goal is to get from the Uncertainty Station to the Certainty Station, and in doing so, they need to have space on one of the tracks to think until they reach certainty.

But track space is limited.

So when there are too many things to think about, we get overwhelmed, and we can struggle to find certainty about anything. (This is normal, by the way. It's just a function of having limited brain space and unlimited needs or interests.)

Now, let's assume there are two or three trains that are always on the track about life stuff. Kids, family, friends. And then there might be some trains that relate to world events, local events, or philosophical things. And then, of course, we have the book.

But the way trains stay on the track is that there is pressure to find certainty. So when we don't have a deadline, or the deadline is flexible, we can often struggle to keep the book on the tracks because there are other things that have more pressure associated with the need for that certainty.

In those cases, especially, we might need the alone time to be able to think over and over something that we're trying to get to the Certainty Station. And that is *still productive time* if it's keeping the trains stalled on the waiting tracks because there needs to be some certainty.

This is also why, on a side note, I often encourage writers who have a high need for internal thought to stay away from social media and the news. When you are voluntarily filling your thought train tracks with things *you have no control over*, you are mucking up your certainty process. Yes, it might be good to be in the know, but I still hold, for most of us, not knowing is better than knowing because when we can't control something, it stresses us out to a point we are never going to get things finished without stress.[1]

Is it actually worth the stress? Most of the time, it's not.

But if you're consistently going on walks, or consistently spending time alone, and you're not able to make yourself think consciously about the book, it's likely there are other trains on the tracks.

We need to clear some tracks so we can get to the book.

Often, when we choose this as the one action we want a writer to take at the end of a coaching session, we'll encourage them to go for a walk a few times without prompts, just to see what happens. See if they can clear off some of the train tracks.

And then, a few days in, we suggest opening the manuscript before you go on the walk and reading the last few pages you've just written to prime the pump.

Sometimes, going on the walk will produce the book thoughts, and I do want to make sure we're always going back to the manuscript and sitting down to see if we can make progress. But honestly, sometimes we just need more time alone. We need to think about other things that aren't the book. Get some of those trains off the tracks.

And if you are wired this way, for the love of everything holy, guard your eyeballs. When you let unnecessary stuff into your head, you will get consumed with it. If more of us spent time intentionally curating what got into our heads, the world would be a better place.

Regardless of the productivity benefits.

(And also, we would be more productive.)

CLARITY DOMAIN: THIS IS ANOTHER CARD that started off in the Clarity Domain, but as I wrote the chapter, I found it being more about removing yourself from the environment of the manuscript (and sometimes from people who have conversational needs) than it was about the manuscript itself. But still, an awful lot of clarity can be reached faster if we regularly give our brains space for quiet.

PROGRESS DOMAIN: IT IS ESSENTIAL THAT WE see walking or driving as progress in the manuscript when we are wired to need this. Even when we want to leave the environment of the manuscript to go to social media or email, we are often responding to the need to be out of the environment of the manuscript. When this happens regularly, it might be worth skipping the social media and going for a walk or drive or bike instead, because that might be the progress we need.

Environment 2

Are there people in your space? Do you need a closed door? Even a closet.

A LOT OF US HAVE LEARNED TO BE MORE reachable than we really need to be, primarily because we live around people who have needs. Because when people need us, it's easiest to do what we are needed for, we don't always ask the question, "Is it good for me to be so accessible to everyone?"

If you aren't creating space from the people who need you, you will burn out. One hundred percent of the time. So in reality, this is just as much a protection of them as it is a protection of you.

But when we are wired to be responsive to our environment (to care about stability or peace), we can't just ignore that wiring. We have to work with it.

And if you know having people in your environment will keep you from writing, then we have to do everything we can to protect you from the people while you're writing.

This might be an office or a bedroom with a closed door. It might be a closet where no one will think to look for you. It might be you going out into the garage and sitting in your car. It might be leaving the house.

There are a lot of options here because the goal doesn't necessarily have to be leaving the actual house. But sometimes, you do need to leave the house.

When your family won't honor your boundaries (if they're too small, or they haven't been trained that no-means-no yet), it either becomes time to train them, or it becomes time to leave the house.

And this is one of those places I get uncomfortable giving advice because, of course, I know some of us are genuinely stuck in situations where we can't just leave the house, and no one is falling over themselves offering to help.

Then we must ask for help. From someone.

It might be a local friend or another parent. It might be a partner, spouse, or parent. It might be an older sibling.

And this isn't just about children. I've coached writers whose animals and adult roommates (or romantic partners) are just as demanding as anyone's children.

This is about having people (or animals) in your physical space when you are being distracted by them constantly.

And no, not everyone can multi-task. So this becomes even more important when your need for a calm environment comes from a place of single-task orientation. When I can only focus without distraction, I have to be aggressive in how I protect that.

Environment 3

Go eat something. Honestly, make a snack and come back to the manuscript in a hot second.

Speaking of things we'd prefer not to do.

On my Facebook page recently, I asked the audience, "If there were no consequences, what is one thing you would quit?"

The number of people who said, "Cooking," was astounding to me. Not because I disagreed, but because I had never realized until that moment just how stressed I got about having to take the time to prepare food.

After I asked that question, I started paying attention to how my stress levels would go up when it was time to break from work and go make a meal (or a snack) and I was so annoyed by the fact that I had to do this again, I was pretty dumbfounded.

Now at least, I can laugh at myself, and how much I hate the fact that we can't just eat one time for the whole week and then never eat again. But many of us need regular calories (or nutrients) enough that we are feeling pain in our physical bodies, and we're not aware it is distracting us from being able to focus.

I'm not talking about hunger.

I'm talking about hangry. That space where you're so hungry, or craving something so much, you're actually mad about it.

It's amazing how many things can be solved by paying attention to our biology and knowing why our bodies are doing what they're doing.

I promise, I'm not trying to get anyone to do healthy eating, because that's a choice we each have to make for ourselves. But I'm just going to put this here as a reminder, as well:

What we eat is sometimes as important as the fact *that* we eat. If I'm getting hangry, that might not be the time for a Snickers bar. (Sorry, Snickers.)

We spend so much time trying to figure out how to hack our productivity, and we ignore one of the largest sources of potential blockage that exists: how our brain functions. If our brain is foggy or dehydrated, or if we're not feeding ourselves food that supports brain health or brain function...

I really need to stop because I'm not trying to dispense advice about how to eat. I just want us to ask the question, "Is what I'm eating supporting brain health, or is it just what my dopamine receptors want me to consume?"[1]

Again. Even if you eat something unhealthy, sometimes the best option is just to eat something, because your body needs the sustenance to do this work.

Environment 4

**When was the last time you had a glass of water?
You're not a cactus, Aidy.**

AND SPEAKING OF BRAIN HEALTH...

I get that there's a cultural fascination among writers with coffee and alcohol. But please, for the love of everything holy...

DRINK SOME WATER, PEOPLE.[1]

Environment 5

Is something off about your environment? Do you need to fix/clean something?

WHEN WE ARE WIRED TO NEED THINGS TO BE in order, or need things to be clean, it's not uncommon for unclean or broken things to distract us enough that we do need to fix or clean them.

This need usually has tells. We'll be thinking about the room or the area, and we won't be able to stop thinking about it. In that case, I would just go and take care of it.

In fact, sometimes, the most productive thing we can do is clean our house, vacuum, wash, fix, because that's also providing us with other progress (potential train track clearing opportunities, as well), and we desperately need that.

Just know, if you need to go handle something, handling it is not always resistance. Sometimes, you really do need to take care of the things to clear your mind.

(This "really quick clearing of the mind" does not apply to: email, social media, news, or text messages. Unless you have an emergency you need to check in on, with your text messages; but generally, all those things would be better off waiting (can you not wait an hour to find out what's new on social media?).

But you won't always benefit from waiting when it's physical environment.

Environment 6

When was the last time you left the house? Maybe leave the house right now, Harry.

ESPECIALLY FOLLOWING MARCH 2020, MANY OF us have gotten quite used to staying in our homes. That's understandable, and of course, I always want us to be safe. But also, we can't not leave the house.

Breathing fresh air (even if it's cold fresh air) is part of the environment of our body. And our body's environment often needs more health consideration than we're consistently giving.

When was the last time you got Vitamin D outside?

When was the last time you breathed fresh air?

When was the last time you went for a drive or a walk?

I'm fully aware that some of us can't leave whenever we want, and some of us have anxiety that keeps us inside more often than not. Again, be safe, but I'm going to encourage us to safely leave the house.

Most writers have some kind of "new and different seeking" personality. There are a lot of traits this can come from, but it is an actual need we have. And so many writers, during the pandemic, got stuck or stalled only because they weren't regularly getting new and different changes to their physical environment.

When we need new-and-different stimulation, we need it.

Leave the house, Harry.

Environment 7

**Where is your current scene set? Can you go there?
Or go somewhere that reminds you of the place?**

NOT EVERYONE IS A SENSE-OF-PLACE WRITER. I get that. Feel free to ignore this if it doesn't align with what you need.

But some of us write very clearly from a sense of place. The need to be physically in a place in order to write it is quite high for some of us. Especially because we're writing real physical spaces.

I recently moved from the mountains to the lake country, and while all my books used to be set in the mountains, I've found myself unable to write those books anymore. When I go outside, I'm constantly taking in data about where I'm located and all that detail makes it into my books.

I've learned about myself that if I get stuck, I often need to either go research the physical location where the scene is set, or I need to go to a place that reminds me of the location. I had a favorite coffee shop I used to frequent that was the inspiration for the bakery I wrote about. The small town my sleuth lived in was a combination of different parts of small towns around me.

And now that I live in a new place, I know I need to go exploring this area, because all my books are probably going to be set here.

Even if you don't write about the physical location where you live, you can still be a sense-of-place writer. It just means you're going to need to understand the environment you're writing about, as much as you need to know the characters.

Just try it.

If you're writing a scene set on a busy street, go to a busy street.

If you're writing about a trek through a forest, go to the forest.

If you're writing about a dungeon, go visit a house with a basement or a historic site with an actual dungeon.

It seems crazy to some people to suggest that being surrounded by details will help the writing at all (and I know writers who are very judgmental about the research trips other writers take, only because they don't need the trip themselves). But if you're a person who writes like this, try changing your environment to the one closest to what you're currently writing.

Environment 8

Take a nap. Yup. That's the whole card, Kevin.

I FEEL LIKE THIS IS SELF-EXPLANATORY. SO I won't say much about it, other than this.

One of the most common questions I get asked is how to be able to write after work. Or how to create space for writing when other things are happening that cause a rise in emotions.

Almost always, I start with two things: showers and naps.

Our minds do clear more as we sleep, so there's part of that. Also, sometimes the act of waking up can create a sense of new beginning.

But additionally, some of us are really tired, and we just need more sleep than we're getting. (We are literally doing too much.)

Not all of us are nappers, and I get that. But if you have ever been helped by a nap before, and you're struggling to stay awake, set a timer for 20 minutes and see if you can sleep.

Just see if it makes a difference.

Environment 9

Are there people interrupting you? Try putting a white board on your door and closing it. That way, people can write what they need on the board, and not have to bother you, and still get their needs met!

THIS IS BY FAR THE MOST COMMON PIECE OF advice I give to parents that has been helpful to protect writing time.

Not all of us can just clear our environments of people, and we can't always leave the house. But there are ways to make sure you're not disturbed.

First, you do have to train people to do this. Not everyone is naturally wired to respect other peoples' boundaries. And training sometimes requires teaching them skills, which can often require the pain of the learning curve.

Second, you have to hold the line. If you say, don't bother me unless there's blood, and they come in to ask you what's for dinner, you have to hold the line. "Is there blood, Jody?" They won't learn to honor the boundary if you don't hold the line.

I know, that's harsh. But that's why people don't honor boundaries. We don't teach them to honor them. (And again, this applies less to little children who haven't had the chance to learn yet. But when kids get old enough, they get the opportunity to learn these things.)[1]

This is why I suggest the white board to almost all parents. Assuming your children are big enough to write on it, of course (and when they aren't, I recommend getting support with someone else watching them while you write, to protect this).

Here's the process.

1. Get a white board for your door with a marker. Tie the marker to the board so it's always there.

2. Instruct the family to write down everything they need to talk to you about or ask you about. Promise that when the door is closed, you will come and find them as soon as you're done.

3. Honor your word. When you're done, open the door and go to talk to them about their white board questions.

A white board on the door allows them to discharge their question or their request without having to bother you, and it allows you to work without disruption.

Win-win.[2]

Environment 10

Switch the direction you face when you're writing. Try a different room if you're able.

I COMMONLY TELL A STORY ABOUT A CLIENT I coached who was "waking up angry" and we got to the bottom of the situation by going through her environment one step at a time until we got to the thing she was really frustrated with.

The part I never talk about is the fact that she did actually change a lot about her environment in the process. She cleaned, she re-painted, she re-decorated.

Each time she would say, "I'm still waking up angry," we would start talking about her environment again, and we would find a new thing that was stressing her out.

So she would fix that thing.

We eventually found that having the blinds open was the trigger for the frustration, and that was specifically because seeing the house behind her brought up an unfixable, unresolved anger that was so subliminal, she wasn't even aware of it.

But it's important to note that we tried to fix everything. She thought it was the room not being clean. It wasn't that.

She thought it was the dingy, dirty walls. It wasn't that.

She thought it was the old furniture. It wasn't that.

The thing that stressed her out the most was something she looked at that she wasn't even aware stressed her out.

This is why one of the Environment advice pieces is to switch the thing you look at. Sometimes, we're really unaware of how our environment impacts us, to the point that we sublimate it.

If you are stuck, consider writing elsewhere. Or just move your desk around. Or if you're like me, where I am right now, I moved to the other side of the table. I used to look out over an empty playground, and on the other side of the table, I can see a little pond and the sunrise.

Even that tiny shift helped me to get unstuck in this book.

Again, environment can be such a big deal.

Even if you're convinced it won't make a difference, just try it. See what happens if you change something about what you look at.

Also, just another quick note on changing environment.

The last house I lived in, I had to keep my blinds closed all the time. After living in my same house for ten years, I realized that all the neighbors around me were 18 years old (I lived in a college town) and they were constantly outside.

I didn't know any of them, and it distracted me to have people looking into my house all day. Plus, I lived on the ground floor, so I was always security conscious. (Drunk college kids get into a lot of trouble, and I'm fine with that. I'd just prefer it wasn't my window they were trying to crawl into, thinking it was theirs.)

My blinds were down 100% of the time. And I didn't realize how bad that was for my mental health until the pandemic. I'd left my house so often in the past, I noticed it less. But when I was in my house all the time, it got really obvious that I wasn't happy in my environment.

I know not everyone has the luxury to be able to move, and I apologize if this frustrates you, so I will be careful of how I say this.

Even the tiniest subconscious environmental barriers can impact us and how we write. This isn't about pretty flowers or painted walls. It's about how your current environment supports your creativity. And yes, I get that not all of us can change our environment completely. So I want to be aware of the fact that 100% change is often impossible.

But even tiny changes like facing the other direction or putting up a screen or a sheet or going out on the deck (or, of course, leaving the house) can be a huge benefit to our environmental sensitivity.

Just a consideration.

Environment 11

Travel.
I know, Ali. I know.
But you may need to travel. Post hasty.[1]

NOT ALL TRAVEL NEEDS TO BE ACROSS THE world, first of all. Much of the travel I suggest in coaching is across the street or across town.

Yes, if you are able to travel longer distances, I usually recommend it because, again, such a high percentage of writers have some kind of "new and different seeking" personality.

But if you're not interested in long trips, I'm also fine with that. The primary goal is just to get you to leave your known environment. This might mean leaving your neighborhood (if you live in a larger city) or leaving your city.

This isn't about rules, it's about principles.

By nature, when we need new and different experiences to give us energy, that requires travel of some kind.

So many people that I coached through the pandemic were struggling with this and as soon as they could safely leave their immediate environment, their block and stuck was helped.

Sometimes it really is as easy as that thing it "can't possibly be."

Environment 12

Go outside. Don't take your phone or computer. Just go outside.

TOO OFTEN, THE ENVIRONMENTS THAT STRESS us out the most are the ones we feel the most addicted to.

Your computer is an environment. It has a system, and that system is likely self-sustaining (meant to keep you in distraction loops and using the equipment until it wears out or needs an upgrade).

You phone is an environment. It is designed to keep you using it. The number of apps available, the colors, the ease, the notifications. It is designed to keep us using it.

If you're not spending significant time away from both these environments, you definitely need to start.

And if the only thing you take away from this book is to more regularly put the phone down, I will consider that a victory.

Phones are the #1 cause of unproductivity in existence.

The very fact that we feel so attached to them and can't live without them is a signal to just how much of our lives they run. And I mean *run*. If you try to start spending less time on your phone, your whole system will rebel against you. Your brain wants the dopamine.

Again. I'm not anti-technology. I just think we don't examine our connection to something, it can control us, and that never ends well.

Go outside.

Environment 13

How long have you been sitting down? Can you stand up? Lay on your back?

THE LAST IMPORTANT PIECE OF OUR environment is our physical body. And I know I'll get some internal pushback from some of you on this one because you would love nothing more than to stay completely disconnected from your physical body so you don't have to think about how much it's failing you. Or how hard you've been on it. Or how it's paying the consequences for past decisions or for having illness or for just getting older.

None of us want to spend significant time thinking about this. And some of you are already skipping this part because you want so badly to not have to think about it.

But if we aren't conscious of the physical container that our consciousness comes in, eventually that physical container will force us to become conscious.

I'd rather see us take preemptive care of the physical body so it can last us a long time.

This is a personal struggle for me because I really like to work. I like to stay seated and push through and get the work done. That also often makes me want to eat the easy food, rather than stop to prepare the healthy food. And it makes me not want to exercise as much because… all that stuff I could get done.

But being disconnected from my physical body has caused me so much pain in the last few years. It's made me much more conscious of the container of my consciousness.

And now I'm doing everything I can to make sure I'm staying more present to my body, including standing up as often as I can. I stretch out my back at least twice a day. I move my body (which is becoming more and more important, the older I get). I do everything I can to maintain my work flow, but not at the expense of my health.

Yes, absolutely, it has a cost. It costs me time and flow sometimes, to get up and walk around. To drink water. To cook healthier food. To work out. It costs.

But it's a cost I'd rather pay.

Again, I don't want to try to force anyone to make choices they aren't prepared to make. I just want to make sure we're aware where the choices we're making are leading us.

Even if it's just small steps (even just getting up, or doing the YLTW posture stretches every hour). I'd rather see small steps than no steps. And if food or exercise is too big a hurdle right now, just do one thing to preserve or strengthen your physical body.

It is your most important environment.

Earlier, when I explained the distinctions between the six domains, I mentioned that progress was about forward motion, and specifically the fact that some things *have* to be done before the words can be written.

Too often, productivity books and writer's block workshops are so focused on getting words on the page, they miss the fact that if we could get words on the page, we would.

But there are things that need to happen in order to produce the words that need to get onto the page.

This domain is all advice regarding how to create progress when I'm not just able to sit down at the computer and start writing words.

Some of it will seem like the proverbial exit off the productivity highway. Trust me, all those miles are actually on the novel highway. Just because they aren't words doesn't mean they are unnecessary.

If all you do is try some of these things out, that's all I ask.

Progress 1

Take a shower. You think I'm kidding. Go get in the shower, George.

ADDITIONAL DOMAIN: CLARITY

This was the first card I printed. I had to do some test cards and I wanted to give something away to the people I saw at this conference I'd attended, who had backed the Kickstarter.

When I handed this card out at the signing table, to a person, everyone laughed and made a joke about writers and hygiene.

I hadn't even considered the hygiene thing when I made this card, so I guess it has a double meaning. You stink, George, take a shower.

But actually, this was a **Progress** card. Not an environment card.

If you need better hygiene, that's between you and your four walls. I'm more concerned with what's going on in your brain.

I'm constantly amazed that more authors don't go directly to the shower when they get stuck, given the **high** propensity of writers who say they get their best ideas in the shower.

So… we don't see the correlation there?

We're alone, we're doing a rote task, no one is talking to us, we can let our mind wander, and we can come to understand things more naturally. I feel like this is too easy.

But when we're stuck, and we are process-to-clarity people, then so often, the next step we need to take is some kind of pro-thinking move. Showers seem to solve multiple problems.

Let's maybe shower more?

CLARITY DOMAIN: I FEEL I'VE PRETTY thoroughly covered how thinking can lead to clarity. Showering leads to thinking.

Progress 2

Is your outline (if you have one) wrong? Do you need to diverge or abandon? (This is perfectly normal and you can still write great books, even when you diverge from your outline!)

OBVIOUSLY, NOT EVERYONE OUTLINES THEIR books, nor should they. But when authors use an outline, we do see several very different ways of using the outline. And all can be successful.

When you are a person who sticks to your outline:

Getting stuck is more often situational or environmental than story-relevant, unless something major has happened to change the character that you didn't anticipate. The other thing that sometimes happens is that you read or hear something another author did that feels too similar to what you've done.

When that happens, it's usually such an anomaly of an occurrence, it can take some time to readjust. Know, this is normal. When we lay a lot of tracks, it can be painful to know those tracks have to be pulled up and re-worked, and the resistance is almost always about not feeling that it's "progress." But when the tracks need to come up, no amount of wishing they didn't is going to make it okay. Better to more quickly move to pulling up tracks and putting down new ones.

When you are a person who uses the outline for the first half:

We see this more often with character-driven writers, so this is often an adapted coping mechanism for the fact that we can't fully know the characters at the beginning of the novel or story. Authors who work like this will almost always start off feeling like they can't write because they have to outline, but then they hit a point where the story lays out and they can see it.

They start writing. But then they diverge from the outline. Often, they don't feel a desire to re-outline from the middle (or wherever they diverged) because the outline was only a tool for getting them started. This is normal and we don't want to worry about this. The best way to proceed is to learn what your triggers are and get to a point in your process where you can trust yourself.

When you are a person who re-outlines at every turning point:

We almost always see this happen because the writer comes up with a better or more interesting story while they're writing. The most important part of alignment here is to make sure to see this re-outlining as an asset. The better story comes about specifically because you wrote the original version.

The way this feels from the inside is a certainty that the story is too predictable if you keep it the way it is. The change is always intended to keep the readers on their proverbial toes.

Benefit.

But you also need to see it as a benefit so you don't guilt yourself through the process.

When you are a person who outlines, then writes, then outlines:

This short-term outlining often happens with people who have used outlines in other ways above, but have learned that they don't need the full outline in order to progress.

Sometimes they need the ending, and sometimes they can't know the ending. But the key is, seeing ahead for short bursts, and then going back to the objective big picture and moving forward.

When you get stuck, it's usually because you're switching so often between big picture and small picture. The in-the-weeds to in-the-clouds transition often needs intentional catalyzing.

If you're writing, go back to the outline. If you're outlining, go back to the writing. Use the one to solve the other.

When you are a person who outlines, and doesn't write a single word of that outline:

We see this the most with New York published writers who have to turn in outlines in order to get contracts. Thankfully, nearly all the writers I've encountered who do this have agents and editors who know the story is going to be good, even when it doesn't follow the outline. But that can be disconcerting.

Just know you're not alone here, if this is you, and you don't need to be different from how you are. You just need to make sure the people who support you in your career know how you function best so they can give you the support you need.

It's important to note that none of these is *the correct* way to write. They're all correct, because they're all aligned with the personalities of the writers who use them. We don't need to change our systems just because they don't align with other people. Those other people don't have to sit down behind your computer screen and write your books, so their system has no relevance to yours.

And this doesn't even touch the fact that many writers don't outline at all. And they can still write well-structured, interesting books that readers love.

Outlining is not righteous.

But it is also not unrighteous. Just know that it's possible to be successful writing with or without outlines.

Progress 3

Go for a drive. Just get in the car and drive somewhere and let your mind wander.

THERE ARE SEVERAL COMPANION CARDS TO each other in the Progress domain that are all about going to do something active so your brain can process. So I'm not going to re-hash every time why this is necessary. Instead, I'll try to layer on from Progress One.

The type of activity you do to make progress matters.

I always think of your available cognitive processes as having a 100% meter, and every activity you do requires a certain percentage of conscious thought and a certain percentage of subconscious thought. (This is completely excepting all the actual unconscious thought.)

When you are driving (in a familiar and safe location), a high percentage of your thoughts that keep you on the road and keep your car operating are subconscious. I don't know the exact math here, but let's just say more than 50%. You could be doing other things in the car while you're driving.

Hence why we have such a high percentage of distracted driving fatalities.

Don't text and drive, by the way.

But because safe driving requires less conscious thought, it allows us to have a higher percentage of our brain available for thinking. (Again, remember the train tracks—thinking counts as working even if it isn't necessarily thinking about the book because we need to move those thought trains to certainty.)

One of the easiest ways to get thinking brains spurred into action is to give them an activity to do that doesn't require a ton of conscious thought. Driving is one of those.

In fact, something I regularly encourage clients to do is to read a segment of their book (especially one that is being problematic) and then go for a twenty minute drive.

And of course, this was a much easier thing to do when the price of gas wasn't so high, so let me just say, going for a walk can almost always fill the same need.

Progress 4

That part you want to skip... can you skip it? Just try making a new copy of the book and taking it out.

IN OTHER LOCATIONS IN THIS BOOK, I WILL SAY "Just because you find it boring does not, in fact mean that readers will find it boring" and I stand by that. For the average writer, maybe this is true. But so many of us have an extremely high new-and-different need (much higher than any reader will ever have), and we judge ourselves for things being boring when, in fact, they aren't.

However.

There's a different kind of "boredom" intuition that I always want to check out. This will not be a regular occurrence, by the way. If you constantly think your books are boring, this is not for you.

This is for those of us who do not always get bored. But we have an intuition about skipping a part of the outline or the manuscript that won't quit nagging at us.

In fact, a large portion of people who bring this up in coaching will admit that they've been wanting to skip. My suggestion is always to try skipping it if your intuition is telling you to skip it.

Especially if it causes you more than a day's worth of being stuck.

Progress 5

Play a video game. It's not procrastination, Jason, it's thinking time. Just do it.

THERE'S A GUY ON YOUTUBE NAMED JIMMY Rees who does these hilarious skits about "The Guy Who Decides" things. The setup is a very out of touch inventor character who's being assisted by a guy named Jason (who is always the logical one).

Every time I say the name Jason, I think of Jimmy Rees' Inventor getting so testy with Jason because the logical brain can't follow the rules of the decision tree he's making up. To The Guy Who Decides, the rules always make complete sense.

So, Jason, in this instance, is definitely said with that Inventor's frustration.

In fact, if you want to pause this book to go watch "The Guy Who Decides Imperial Measurements" so you can get the full Jason voice, I will wait.

Video games are one of the most maligned "procrastination" devices among writers. Not a surprise that many of us are attracted to video games as a pastime because they are story based. But this idea that video games are always of no use needs to get debunked.

First of all, as we've said in other chapters, we need to have some activities that don't use 100% of our conscious brain space because we often need that space for thinking.

Second, the story-based nature of games can sometimes help jar loose the storytelling in our novels (and not always only because of the actual events; sometimes, it's the structure of those events).

Third, and I say this in full Jason-Jason-Jason mode: Not. All. Progress. Through. The. Book. Is Writing. Words. Jason.

However.

I understand completely the fear that if you start playing video games all the time, you'll just be playing video games and not writing. And that's a valid fear.

Video games are easier than writing.

And for those of us who are wired to be fun-seekers, writing might not ever be as fun as video games, even in its best moment.

So, how do we manage the video games and keep them from becoming an addiction or an avoidance?

1. Never play video games first. When we go to the video games first, we set up our dopamine receptors to want more of that craic. So this should be a hard and fast rule if you're using them for processing.

(Unless: there is one important caveat. I have several clients who play rote games in the morning for a very specific amount of time, but those people can always make themselves disconnect from the games and switch into writing mode. If you've never successfully been able to make yourself switch, then don't put yourself in that place regularly.)

2. Always try another thinking activity first if you can.

3. Set a timer to get up from the game (or end the game), and even if you plan to return to the game, stand up and walk away when the timer goes off. Some of us can feel when we're ready and when we're not, and it's important to know that you can return if you need to, but get yourself into the habit of not treating the games as inertia.

4. Open the manuscript when you're finished and see if you can make progress.

5. If you go to bed after the game, wake up the next morning and open your manuscript, to see if you can make progress. If you can't, no worries. But...

6. Don't go right back to the games if you can't make progress. Make yourself do something else for a time. The more we go back to the games and don't ask if we can make progress, the more likely we are to just be playing them for the addiction and not for the progress.

And as always, some of you know that video games are only safe for you if they're play-time activities because you know your addiction capacity is high. If you're this person, and you've set a hard rule for yourself around video games and productivity, I'm fine with that.

You should skip this card.

For the rest of us, at least try this out. Just see if it helps. Sometimes, the relaxation alone or the focus on fixing a different problem can shift the way we're thinking about our writing.

Progress 6

What if you killed a side character right now?
Sometimes, murder is the answer, Jen.

ADDITIONAL DOMAIN: Surprise

If you are heavily anticipatory in your personality, you are likely the kind of person who looks ahead in your writing. Even when you're not aware of it.

Often, these anticipatory personality types get stuck when there's something ahead of them or behind them that needs changing. The problem is, your brain won't just tell you, "Oh, hey, Jen... just so you know... you should have killed that guy back there at the bus stop."

No. Because it's an annoying little thing.

It hides the thing it knows, like a little game of cat and mouse. It wants you to come play and figure it out. How fun, right?

Only it's not fun.

Most of us are deeply annoyed when our brain does this, and we need the surprise of "try this" specifically to see how our brain will react to that change.

If you've ever been brainstorming with a friend, and you are this type of person, you are likely to shoot down all the ideas they give you because the ideas won't work for your story. In fact, many of us feel bad about this because we feel we "should" be using the ideas when we're brainstorming.

Instead, I highly recommend just preparing your brainstorm partner ahead of time.

Say something like this:

"You know I find our brainstorm times so helpful. My brain just has this weird thing where it hides stuff from me, and I have to chip away at it with ideas. So even if I'm shooting ideas down, please know, it's not because I think they're bad ideas. It's because there's this one very specifically shaped idea that's going to make the story work, but I can't find it myself. I am deeply annoyed by this. I wish I wasn't this way. Also, I appreciate your help more than I can say. I can only imagine how frustrating it must be to have someone shoot down literally every idea, and I'm so grateful you continue to do this with me. You are such a good friend."

Then you've set their expectations around helping you to be accurate to the situation. They can feel helpful, and you can still get the help you need.

But let's be honest. Most of you aren't going to do this. You still feel guilty for shutting ideas down. So you need other support.

It's much harder to do this level of progress for yourself. Sometimes, it really is necessary to bring in another person. But in the next few cards, we're going to talk about some ways to get yourself into that shift of perspective on your own.

The first is:

Kill someone.

In the book, Jen. Not in real life. But the decision to kill someone in the book makes your anticipatory brain have to come up with all the different reasons why you can't kill them.

Or, you kill them and it changes the story trajectory.

Either way, you have progress.

Progress 7

What's the thing you want to do but you think is stupid? It's not stupid. Just do the thing your intuition is telling you to do, no matter what it is.

WRITERS HAVE A LOT OF INTERNAL resistance around following intuition. I know this is normal. I just think it's worth pointing out, many of us can look back at our track record with following our intuition and see how it worked out for us in the past.

Often, the thing we intuit needs to happen is really the thing that needs to happen, and we just need to try doing that thing.

If it helps at all, there is a reason we have this internal voice that's trying to convince us not to listen to our intuition. It's usually trauma-related. But there is a reason. That voice is trying to be helpful. It's just not.

Many of us who are highly intuitive need to practice saying no to the critical voice that's been trying to protect us from doing stupid things or from making mistakes. In fact, there's growing research in emerging psychological fields that suggests most of the critical voices we hear inside are coping mechanisms and can be ignored.

Not all. We still want you to have a conscience.

But many of those voices are just parts of us that have developed to help us cope with the world and exist in a way that experiences less friction. Again, I can't recommend Internal Family Systems therapy enough to people.

There are small ways to experiment with saying no to these critical voices. One of them is to write the thing in the book you think will be stupid. Just to let someone else validate for you that the voice is wrong. Turns out, it was exactly the right thing the story needed.

Turns out your intuition was right.

I'm not surprised.[1]

Progress 8

Alex suggests: Side load your WIP to your Kindle and read through it in a comfy chair as if you were a reader. Let your brain make predictions and form ideas of where to go as you read.

ADDITIONAL DOMAINS: CLARITY, RESOURCE

This was one of our Kickstarter advice additions, and it's such a great one because it fits so well into the Progress domain.

I'm not sure if Alex does this only at the end of the project, but I would suggest this piece of advice in multiple different places.

1. At turning points. Often, when we change direction in the book, we need to look back and see how we laid the groundwork for things, or how we had loops open. When we stall out at turning points, re-reading the manuscript can be very crucial.

2. In the middle. Many writers get stuck around 45-60% of the way through the book specifically because of the number of open loops. When this is the case, the only way to know for sure that you've gotten all the open loops to close is to actually re-read the text.

We talked about this a bit in the **Clarity** domain as well, so go back and read that if you need more thoughts here.

(Although, to be fair, some of us just keep writing and let our editor find the open loops, and that is also reasonable. As long as you know for sure your editor will/can find them. But if you have an editor who can't find open loops... do you need a new editor? Maybe.)

3. When you are actively stuck. This is how I imagine Alex meant the advice, as well, because I asked everyone for tips on getting unstuck. I love the idea of using the Kindle, which is why there's a **Resource** domain attached to this, as well.

Previously, I would always suggest printing the pages so you could walk away from the computer, but loading onto the Kindle or tablet gets us to the same destination. The important part here is not to read in the same medium you write in. So if you're in Scrivener, make sure you're compiling. If you're in Word, make sure you're printing or Kindling. Just change the medium.

It helps your brain think differently.

Great advice, Alex. Thank you!

Progress 9

Have you tried moving on to a new project for a time? Just to see if this current work needs to percolate?

ADDITIONAL DOMAIN: SURPRISE

One of the most commonly given pieces of advice in the writing community is to *never leave the manuscript*.

And if you've known me for even half a hot second, you know I like to question the premise of any commonly-given advice just to make sure it's worth listening to for any one individual person.

Often, the advice isn't worth most people listening to.

That doesn't make it bad advice. It works for the person who's giving it. And it works for other people who are like them (or similar enough that it will actually solve the problem). But let me say this a little louder.

Not all advice is worth listening to.

This is why I caveat and explain the "why" behind all the advice in this book. I couldn't just let the advice stand on its own. I needed to tell you why it works and why it might not, so you can be a better decider for yourself about whether or not to use it.

As I used to say in every episode of the QuitCast, "Anyone can tell you what works for them, and they can say *it might not work for you*, but they can't tell you why. I can tell you why."

So when I question the premise (QTP) some very commonly given advice like this, I want to make sure to explain why it works and why it might not work.

When someone says, "Don't leave the manuscript," they're trying to help solve the problem of resistance. And this is where a lot of the writing advice in our community comes from.

Trying to solve the resistance problem.

For some people, resistance is just something to be passed through.

But for some of us, that resistance is telling. Useful. Helpful. In fact, for some of us, resistance is quite literally the signal that we should leave the manuscript.

When we have a personality that makes us want to do things the right way (which, of course, not everyone has), we can often follow advice that isn't meant for us just because it is commonly repeated.

So I want to ask you, about the previous books you've written where you've ignored the desire to leave the manuscript:

How has that gone for you?

If you find yourself having to eventually leave the manuscript anyway, then let's just give you the permission to leave the first time you have the instinct, rather than the fiftieth. Save ourselves fifty hours or fifty days.

The problem is, the people giving the "Don't leave the manuscript" advice can't imagine needing to actually leave the manuscript. For them, the resistance is always worth pushing through. Either they like the pain of the push, or the resistance is not a signal.

But if you are a person who experiences resistance and you need to listen to it, because you want a better book, and your brain will eventually make you listen to it. You'll just feel insane piles of guilt when you do, because you think you're doing it wrong.

Just go ahead and leave the manuscript.

Switch to a new project.

There is nothing inherently righteous about not switching projects. This idea that if you switch, you'll never finish is based on an assumptive premise that everyone is wired to make progress linearly and coherently on only one project at a time.

Oh, my sweet summer child.

Winter is coming.

Or rather, winter is here and I've seen it and you should just switch to a different manuscript.

Because with people who are not wired for that linear, coherent, one-time-through-the-book process, they will not be helped by staying. Following the energy of the story will help them make progress in multiple places and finish all the manuscripts, eventually.

That's the key.

If you are wired to switch between projects, you'll find that you finish the same number of books in a one-year period as the person who doesn't do one book at a time. And for sure, you'll finish more books in a one year period by switching than you would if you forced your way through only one project at a time.

In fact, writers who are wired this way will often get so stuck trying to force themselves to just stay inside the manuscript, they can do damage to their progress. So. Please. Just question the premise of the advice.

Even if the only question you ask is: how's that working out for you in the long run?

That's enough.

Progress 10

Stop writing for the day. Tonight, before you go to sleep, write on an index card where your story should go next. Ask your sleeping brain to help you.

ADDITIONAL DOMAIN: Clarity

When we hear advice about writer's block and stuckness, I think it's important that we hear the word "stop" sometimes.

Sometimes, progress has stop signs, as well.

Most of the reason that a segment of writers fears the blank page is because we innately believe progress has to all be word count related. But sometimes, progress means doing other things. And sometimes, progress means stopping all together.

A major strategy we employ to deconstruct the fear around the blank page is the embracing of the fear of the blank page.

It's important to know that our brains are wired for survival, not for happiness. They are wired to keep us alive, and to get better-faster at keeping us alive successfully.

The response to fear, when it's survival-related, is fight-flight-or-freeze. So in life or death situations, it's normal to freeze or flee when confronted.

But the blank page is not life or death.

The best thing we can do for our brains when it comes to both progress and also the blank page is to embrace the fear of the blank page. In this case, fear is not a signal that you're in danger.

We have to tell ourselves that. Regularly.

The blank page is not dangerous. This is just our brain responding in survival mode. But we're safe. The blank page is a good thing. I have skills and tools that can help me move past the blank page.

The problem is, of course, when we let fear drive the motorcycle, it's going to steer us away from the blank page, or it's going to freeze us so badly, we won't be able to even sit down in front of it.

But fear of the blank page is a good thing when the blank page isn't actually dangerous. We get into a rhetorical question asking fiasco and we end up in nonstop freeze.

What if I can't do this? What if I can never write again? What if the story won't come? What if? What if?

And if we are afraid enough of that blank page, we will absolutely kick into survival mode in our fear, and we will 100% freeze up.

The problem is, encouragement to "just write the next sentence" or "just sit down and write something" or "stop thinking" only makes that freeze resistance higher.

Stronger.

More frozen.

What we need, in that frozen moment, is the soothing reminder that the blank page is not dangerous. We need to answer those rhetorical questions. And we need to remind ourselves that we have the tools to progress—and whatever tools we don't have, we can find. We know where to go for help.

Answer rhetorical questions.

What if I can't do this?

Answer the question. What if you can't write the first chapter? You'll think about it and it'll come to you. The brain you have, which has written first chapters in the past, is not any different. You still have the same tools you had when you wrote the last book.

What if I can never write again?

The only thing likely to keep me not writing is to continue asking these rhetorical questions, though. Otherwise, I know this is just a fight-or-flight response to fear. But the blank page isn't going to kill me, so there's no reason to be as afraid of it as I would be of a wild lion. It's not going to bite me. I've done this in the past, I can do it again.

(Use your parental voice. Your assured voice. Or go listen to some of my podcasts and hear me say it. Hear my parental voice that I have to use on myself.)

What if the story won't come?

Then I have tools to help me find the story. I now have this Stuck List that I can use to help me find a tool to apply to the situation. There is something in here that will help me to get unstuck. I am not without weapons in this "fight" against the blank page.

Don't allow your brain to ask you so many survival questions ("What if the lion gets me?") that you freeze. The fear is a good thing.

I say all this in the "Stop" chapter because many of us have a similar feeling about stopping writing. We're afraid being stopped is a sign that we're not going to be able to pick back up again.

If you're having a fear of leaving the manuscript, and you find yourself feeling that throat-close of fear, use your parental voice to remind yourself of the following.

"I can pick this back up tomorrow. I'm going to write on this index card where I think the story should go next and that's going to help my sleeping brain think on this."

So often, we have to remind ourselves that there is no actual physical danger in the manuscript. But because there aren't wild lions outside our house anymore, we don't have the actual survival mode problems for reference.

Our poor brains can't tell the difference between the blank page and a lion because we have more relative safety than we would if the lions were actively around and stalking us.

But knowing this can help us have more control over the survival mechanisms.

We need the reminders that there's nothing our manuscript can do that will actually kill us. Not stopping. Not being blank. Not going in the wrong direction. We are not in danger.

Take a deep breath.

Repeat after me.

This book will not kill me.

CLARITY DOMAIN: THIS CARD ORIGINALLY started off in the Clarity domain, but I really needed to make one of the **Progress** cards have the word "stop" in it. But sleep is often one of the places where we can produce clarity, even though it's unintentional. So just make sure you're considering putting the thought in your mind before you go to bed, so you can wake up having thought about it subconsciously all night long.

Progress 11

Have a one-minute dance party. Come on, Cammy! Dance!

I'M HOPEFUL THIS CARD SPEAKS FOR ITSELF. This is one of those "get out of the chair and move your body" cards because inertia is a real thing.

Sometimes, what we need the most is just to change the physical position of our body.

Plus. Who doesn't like a one minute dance party?

And yes, you can dance in your chair. Move the body as much as possible, and throw on some music.

When I do this, I have a "get psyched mix" that I use and I throw it on random so there's some serendipity. But you can do ballet or interpretive, you can do club or hip hop, you can do anything you want.

I just want there to be a change in the inertia.

Progress 12

Call a friend and explain where you are in the story and why you can't proceed. You don't have to take their advice, Joe. And you can thank them for the chat even if you don't take their advice.

BECAUSE WE DISCUSSED A BIT ABOUT THIS IN the Progress 6 chapter, I'm not going to re-hash that entire discussion about how talking can be helpful even if they don't give you actual advice that helps you.

Additionally, some of us are very introverted, and we resist talking about the story for really valid reasons. The only time I would suggest an introvert doing this is when you have genuinely not been able to find help in any other card in this domain.

But some of us are wired to be dialogic by nature, and we resist this advice with every fiber of our being.

"I shouldn't have to talk to someone about my story" is the most common sentence I hear from writers wired in this way.

You shouldn't?

Why?

And let me just say, Joe, if the only reason you think you shouldn't is because other people don't have to... you know what I'm going to say to that.

Other people's process isn't relevant to you.

QTP your shoulds.

If calling someone works every time, then the question isn't "should you call someone?" The question is, "would you rather stay stuck?"

Would you prefer putting someone else out? Or staying stuck? Because you can absolutely stay stuck. If this is a common problem, though, you probably won't be able to just get yourself out of this place. And the key word to the why is in the wiring.

Dialogic.

Dialogue.

Two people.

You can't have a dialogue with yourself. That's a monologue, Jason.[1]

Here's the thing about dialogic wiring: you won't really know what you think until you say it out loud. And worse than that, you will often get halfway into the beginning of the conversation and have already solved the problem just by how you're explaining it to the person.

That's because your brain is wired to make meaning in relationship to other people. When you get stuck in your meaning-making, you need that other person to genuinely listen and be present in order to help you know what you think. But you won't be able to know this is what you think until you get ready to talk about it. Or until you are actually talking about it.

Most of us who are wired like this have also been punished for being this way. We've been shamed for talking too much or we've been made to feel we are too much (or we're worried about being too much because we can see or feel when others hit the overwhelm point with our talking). Knowing this is important because it allows us to give ourselves the freedom of adulthood.

Adulthood is the perspective we couldn't have as kids. Adulthood means that everyone is in charge of their own emotions. If someone feels like we're too much, then they are not for us. And as adults, we can choose to move on to a different friendship. But we often can't do that as children. Especially if the people making us feel this way are our family members or teachers. We don't have the same level of choice there.

But adulthood brings more free choice. We aren't responsible for managing our talking to make everyone comfortable. If they want us to stop talking, they are adults. They can say, "Can we do this another time?" (By the way, that carries the implication that they do want to do this again. Just, in the moment, the overwhelm is a brain wiring thing and they're trying to be helpful in the way they can be.)

And if they are secretly hating our talking and not telling us, they're not being a good adult friend.

Because we talked in a different segment about the overwhelm that can happen to some internal-processing brains when they get too much information, I do want to say: overwhelm is a natural state. It doesn't always mean we're doing something wrong. Sometimes it means it's just time for them to take a break.

This is also why, as a dialogic person, I have multiple friends to talk to, because I know the expectation that one friend should have to listen to me all the time is unrealistic. I need more support than that. And it's amazing how often the answer is, "I need more support than that." To anything.

All this to say, when you have this need, you have this need. Is it worth the pain you'll go through to try not being this way? Or is it better to embrace the way you are and see it as an asset?

I choose to see my dialogic nature as an asset. I've learned to listen better over the years because I know how important it is to be heard. And I can still work on my listening. But not-talking is not the answer.

Progress 13

Is there a different part of the story you know and could write? Move to that part.

NOT ALL OF US CAN SKIP TO A DIFFERENT PART of the story in manuscript words—if you can, this is your reminder to do that.

But even if you can't skip in the manuscript, can you hand-write about the part you can see? Or call a friend and talk about the part you can see? Sometimes, the part you can see will lead you to the part you can't see.

I also understand that not all of us can write out of order, which is why I don't necessarily suggest writing manuscript words (sometimes the writing-in-linear-order also comes with a side helping of can't-erase-words-I've-written, so I want to be conscious of that). But if you can somehow process the part of the story you do know, that can often lead to processing the parts that are hiding themselves from you.

Especially when other cards in Clarity and Progress aren't working.

Progress 14

Do you need to move a preorder? I know, I know. But... do you?

I PUT THIS LAST IN THE PROGRESS DOMAIN because I knew this would be a major pain point for some of us. And I don't like to make people be in pain, no matter how it might seem.

Some of our wiring that is beneficial in other areas really kneecaps us when it comes to adaptation. One of those writing elements is the desire to meet commitments.

I cannot tell you how many people I coached through the first two years of the pandemic that had some version of this story happen.

They set a preorder.

Life goes crazy or changes in an unpredictable way.

They try to make the preorder.

They miss the preorder through no fault of their own.

They feel guilty for not working harder to make the preorder, even though **gestures around at the world on fire** because they think they should have been able to "still get it done, no matter what."

And that wiring—that "get it done no matter what" wiring—is really beneficial. Except when things happen out of your control that do actually keep you from being able to meet your commitments.

Most of the time, when I would coach writers going through this experience, I actually had to walk through every week (and sometimes every day) of their previous several weeks or months in order to prove to them that they couldn't have done it any differently than they did.

Just so they can feel sane about cancelling a preorder.

That's the level of pressure we put on ourselves for fulfilling our expectations (even when we can't).

The problem for progress mostly isn't the preorder itself, it's that when the preorder is missed, we still want to hold ourselves accountable for trying to get the work done when we can't. And we keep trying to catch up, when we really just need to admit that we did our best and things still didn't work out the way we wanted.

And I do apologize if that sounds mean. My intention is always to reflect what would be easiest or best for us, as writers, with the personality we have. And sometimes, the best thing we can do for ourselves is to have a really hard conversation with ourselves about what is realistic and what we can actually expect from ourselves.

When we need to do something like cancelling or moving a preorder in order to have our sanity and get our forward progress back, I just want to make sure we can do that.

PART VI
FIFTH DOMAIN: RESOURCE

One of my strongest natural traits is the collection of resources, so if you know me, you can imagine how hard it was to be limited to only 13 cards in the Resource domain.

But.

I think I've managed it.

The goal of these cards was mostly to get us thinking about picking up specific types of tools to solve specific types of problems. Some of these cards are about character traits and actions. Some of the cards are about classes or workshops. And some are about books. Not everyone is a "go to resource" person first, so if this doesn't resonate with you, feel free to skip.

But my hope is, if you're using this as a way to build your own personal Stuck List (which was the original goal of the book, after all), at least one of these cards (or a similar tool) will make its way into your rotation of un-stuck actions.

And of course, this is a curated list made by an individual person, so it's not comprehensive. But I'll try to give the principle of the reason I'm recommending the tool in each chapter so you can find other similar tools if you don't happen to like the one I'm suggesting.

Resource 1

Do you know your POV character's Top Five Strengths?

OF COURSE, FROM A CERTIFIED STRENGTHS Coach, you're going to get advice about going to the CliftonStrengths© assessment. This language has become part of my DNA.

The assessment itself is a paid tool, so it is definitely not worth doing tests on behalf of your character, but I find it to be very helpful as a way of processing character traits, especially for alignment.

In the construction of the tool, it's important to note that this wasn't something where one person decided "there are four types of people" and then created a test to find those four types. (Those tools can be perfectly valid as discussion topics, that's just not how the Strengths metric was created.)

When Dr. Clifton started his research, he was looking for an explanation to the data he saw. Why is it that successful people are not all successful in exactly the same way? Is there any predictability to the traits that certain types of successful people manifest?

So he went looking. He and his research team interviewed 2 million of the most successful people in the world, over the course of the research (and, by the way, Gallup continues to validate that research over time because they're such data nerds—grateful for that; I love data).

What this means: the patterns were there to find, and he found them. The correlation between certain types of successful behavior was so sharp, and so consistent, he created the 34 Strengths and then the test that would discover those patterns in individual people.

As I said, it's not worth doing a test (the way you could do a Myers-Briggs test or an Enneagram) on behalf of your character because the tool isn't free. But using the outcome can be exceptionally helpful.

My favorite thing to do with Strengths is to look for opposites. I want to find traits that feel like they have some conflict, and then I give them to different characters. In fact, if you use the Discovery Card tool that Gallup publishes (you can find it in the "cards" section on their website store), there is a "contrasting" section at the bottom of those cards.

The cards themselves aren't meant to be a character development tool. But they definitely give the best version of the traits for easy use. I have several sets of Gallup's Strengths cards, and I regularly use them to look at how aligned behaviors look.

Rather than pulling character traits out of a hat, I think using aligned resources like the Strengths or the Enneagram is the most helpful way because it helps to produce realistic characters.

Part of the reason people talk about Strengths and the Enneagram so much, especially in the writing community, is because they are so resonant. The traits are observed patterns in millions of people. And when we've used them in coaching, people often read that individualized report of their 34 traits and feel a little self-conscious about how accurate it is.

(The number of people who ask if I'm spying on them when we do coaching calls is very high.) "How can it be this accurate?" they'll ask me.

And of course, the answer is, "Because they did their homework."

That veracity is the reason I use the Clifton test almost exclusively in individual coaching. The alignment potential is off the charts.

That means, the resonance is off the charts, which means it can help produce aligned characters.

Why aligned characters matter: we naturally sort behaviors in our brains into predictive patterns. In fact, one of our biological survival mechanisms is the desire to understand the behavior of other people. (It's the reason why we are confused by the behavior of other people—we don't have a template for understanding their behavior and that's supposed to help our survival.)

When a character acts in a way that feels recognizable to us, we don't pay attention to it anymore. Biologically, we are wired to be bothered when people's actions don't align with something we recognize. So there's a little subconscious "ick" we feel when that happens.

And of course, we're almost never aware of this. The process itself is so subconscious, we don't make the conscious decisions. They just happen. So when a character isn't aligned (when the personality traits don't seem "normal" to us), we notice it. Whereas, when the traits are aligned, we don't notice. They seem normal. Safe.

This seems strange to some of us who are less conscious of our thought patterns, and I get that. But we even do this to ourselves. Most of our normed behaviors, we don't notice. When we do something that we don't like, or that we judge ourselves for, it's because we don't understand why we do it or where it comes from. (And those are often the questions we ask, as well. "Why can't I just write 4000 words a day, Becca?")

We may not see the subconscious norming, but it's happening. Again, it's a survival mechanism, so it's biological.

Readers do this as well. Without even realizing it. And they are judging the patterns of the characters against the patterns of real people without realizing it, too. When it aligns, they feel good (resonant... biologically safe). When it doesn't align, they don't feel good. That is a signal to their brain that something's wrong.

They won't say, "This character didn't feel aligned."

What they say is, "I didn't like them. They didn't seem real. Their actions don't make sense. I don't believe this."

When you write characters that have aligned personalities (where the traits themselves naturally occur together and are a recognizable pattern that you would see from people), readers can relax and just feel and enjoy the story.

This isn't the only character-based tool I will discuss. But for right now, I think it's important to know that alignment does matter.

And similarly to every other discussion about your writing... you do *not* have to align characters intentionally. It's possible to write aligned characters because you are naturally able to sort behaviors into predictable patterns. And not predictable in a bad way. Predictable in a way that doesn't make readers feel biologically insecure when they're reading. They're not going to be afraid of the book if they feel this unaligned response. They're just going to put it down or not like it.

Also, another caveat: we are recognizing more and more complexity in personality traits and in behavior patterns as we continue to study people. Success psychology is in its infancy still, as a science field (and in general psychology is still just a teenager). There is so much to learn, and I imagine that people using this tool in 100 years will know so much more about the human brain than we know today.

Nuance in patterning becomes more obvious, the harder you look, and just know, I'm not saying there are 34 different kinds of people and only those people are aligned. I'm saying there are 378,000 different kinds of Top Five Strengths combinations, and beyond that, nuance in the Enneagram numbers and MBTI and DISC and Kolbe and every other metric. So there are actually billions of ways to be resonant. We'll discover more and more of that nuance as we move along.

But for now, it's important to know that we are testing personality patterns for resonance and relevance as we read. So tools like this, even though they are made for real people, can be helpful in character creation and realignment.

. . .

QUICK EXERCISE: IF YOU DO END UP GETTING the Discovery cards, or you even just look at your own Full34 report for some of the individual Strengths language, try this exercise:

Take an executing Strength and a relationship-building Strength and pull one of the descriptive words from each. Give two characters in a scene the different traits as their main goal in this scene. Explore how they might disagree or how this main motivation might cause conflict between them, if that one word or trait was their primary goal, and they were trying to help the other person get on their side.

Enjoy!

Resource 2

Open a book from a similar genre to the same page you're on in your manuscript and read that book for two pages.

HOPEFULLY IT GOES WITHOUT SAYING THAT I am not suggesting you copy or plagiarize from other books. And if you are the kind of person who can't help but use language you hear (and you're self-conscious about reading in your own genre so you don't copy), you can ignore this.

But for many of us, when we are stuck, we're having a hard time seeing where to go forward, and we can be helped by looking at how other masterful writers have done something similar.

The first time I did this exercise, I'd heard someone suggest it at a writing conference and get a *huge* amount of pushback for it. So of course, I had to try it out for myself. (Who doesn't love a rebellious personality?)

I was writing a mystery book and I'd gotten stuck in a place about 3/4 of the way in. I could not progress, no matter what.

So I opened one of the Sue Grafton books and turned to the chapter that was the closest to the trajectory of my plot. They eliminated one of the suspects as a suspect.

I didn't want to do that (I liked keeping everyone in tension), so I put the book down and opened a Rhys Bowen book to a similar place. They also eliminated one of the suspects as a suspect there.

I was real big mad now.

So I went to MC Beaton, HY Hanna, Sara Paretsky, Patricia Cornwell, Sara Rosett, Jana DeLeon... you get the picture.

Every single book, when they got to this place, they started eliminating suspects (and most reduced the pool to two final people). I wanted to wait until 7/8 of the way through the book to have any kind of resolution where I eliminated suspects. And I did still wait a little longer than I should have (because I realized by doing this exercise that I still had a thread I had to wrap up before I could fully settle people).

But this taught me a valuable lesson.

When all the great writers of your genre are progressing similarly, there's a reason why they're doing it. What I found I got in feedback about that book (some of which I was able to catch in edits) was that the uncertainty about the large number of suspects was unnerving. It felt like too much to keep in their head, to have four suspects and we never know for sure who *wasn't* the killer until one moment 7/8 through the book.

It also did not allow the reader to know who the killer was, and the more readers feel like you are intentionally hiding things from them, the less they trust you. I needed to learn that.

Since that experience, I regularly pull this suggestion out when I know writers are newer to a genre (even if they've read the genre widely in the past, as I had—I'd been reading mystery and thriller my entire life). When you haven't had to construct plots in this genre, you can sometimes miss those little nuances that you might only see if you can get a bird's eye view of a bunch of different writers.

This can help for big plot things, but it can also help for little things like the revelation of a secret or the deeper knowledge of a character's backstory or the final introduction of a murder weapon, etc.

Watching how the greats do it isn't bad form. And it's not copying. (As long as you don't plagiarize—I hope I don't have to actually say that in a book for writers.) It's patterning.

It's research.

Resource 3

Has someone read the book? Are you expecting yourself to find a problem you can't find? Do you need perspective?

THE FIRST TIME I WENT TO MELBOURNE, Australia, I stayed in a hi-rise hotel in the CBD (Central Business District) that overlooked downtown. And it was stunning. Because of the potential for quarantine upon entering the country, I had to arrive a week early (we were expecting a possible seven-day quarantine if we tested positive for Covid after disembarking the plane), so I wouldn't even possibly miss this very important conference I'd come to the country for.

That meant I did a lot of walking around the city of Melbourne when I didn't test positive. And I loved that city. I spent almost all day, every day, outside walking around the CBD, just loving it. In fact, I spent so much time outside, I felt like I knew every inch of that place. And we had unseasonably good weather for the winter, so it was sunny almost every day.

But one day, near the end of my stay, it rained and I spent a good portion of my morning in my hotel room, with that view.

I was sitting in the window, working, when I started really looking at the neighborhood around me.

Right next door, I saw something that shocked me.

A basketball court!

If you know me, I am a basketball fiend—I played basketball in high school, I've traveled to watch college and pro games, I watch it obsessively in the Formula 1 off-season… I mean, the winter. I usually have a pretty honed radar for basketball courts.

How did I miss a basketball court right next to my hotel?? I was shocked.

When I walked on the street, after the rain stopped, I realized the problem. From the street, because of the angle of the sidewalk, the bushes that hadn't looked particularly high from my hotel room were over my head when I walked along the wall toward my favorite coffee shop. (Axil Coffee, by the way, on Elizabeth Street. So good.)

My pedestrian perspective didn't allow me to see the court for the trees. But when I got up in the hotel room, I could see the court.

This experience gave me the perfect metaphor for why perspective is so important.

As writers, we are not able to get in the hotel room about our story. We are not able to be up high enough above the story that we can look down and see the holes or the problems or the open loops.

This is not because we are stupid or we need to learn something. It's specifically about perspective. We need other people to have perspective on the work we do in order to tell us what's really going on down there.

And sometimes, when we get stuck, the only thing that's going to help us is to get up in the hotel room and look down on the story is someone else's perspective. Someone who isn't down on the pedestrian sidewalk being obscured by bushes.

I often sense this frustration in writers that they can't always fix their own problems, and let me just say... I get this. I get not wanting to need other people. That's valid.

It won't take away the need for other people, but I get the frustration.

We can either be consumed by that frustration and let it keep us from success, or we can give in and ask for help.

There's definitely a choice there, and not all of you will choose to get the perspective. I get that. But I at least wanted to represent the fact that you cannot have perspective on your own story.

You are not capable of getting in the hotel room.

That's why you are getting stuck when there's something wrong. You either need someone to talk to you about the story so you can get a different perspective (which is, again, valid), or you can get someone to read the book or the section you're working on.

Some of us will eventually stumble onto the answer, and if you're the kind of person who prefers to wait until you do, that's also a valid life choice.

I just want to represent that there's a faster way to get that done, in case anyone wants to take the elevator.

Resource 4

Do you need a hard deadline? (Not everyone can meet deadlines they set for themselves, Jillian. Question the premise.)

A LOT OF US GREW UP WORKING TO DEADLINE in school and have acquired an easy pattern of being deadline-driven. And as I've said in earlier parts of this book, I'm a fan of not trying to change things that will take too long to change (and instead, working with how we're already wired in most cases).

So let's assume, if you are deadline driven (or externally motivated), we're just going to work with that for the time being. You can decide if you want to put in the years of work to change it later. For now, let's just assume this is a harder-wired pattern.

Rather than expecting yourself to magically develop internal motivation, how about we just assume you really need a hard deadline?

Preorders. Editorial deadlines. Critique swaps. Something with some teeth in it, where real people have real expectations.

In fact, when I first started consulting on productivity, one of the most common questions I was asked was, "How come I can be so effective at using a planner at the office, but when I get home, I can't make myself do the work?"

I used to be a little incredulous about this (now I have more sympathy, because it happens so often), because of course, they told me why. It's at work. There are consequences. At work, someone is making you do the things.

At home, no one is making you do the things.

The same holds true with book deadlines. When you are not meeting your own deadlines, it doesn't mean you need to want it more. It doesn't mean you don't like your own books. It doesn't mean you're self-sabotaging.

It literally just means you are externally motivated.

So you need external motivation.

Rather than feeling bad about this, just give yourself some external motivation. Find someone to hold you accountable (even if it's a critique swap or a live cowriting or coworking experience). Don't just sit there feeling guilty you're not internally motivated to do your own work. Use that others-motivation to your advantage.

Resource 5

Read an old poem, and insert a line from the poem right into the manuscript where you are right now.

ONE OF MY FAVORITE THINGS ABOUT PICKING up a new book for the first time to read is the epigraph. When there is one, of course.

It's why there are epigraphs in all my mystery books.

Being inspired by the words of other writers is a major theme in my learning development. Almost every time I pick up an old poem, I find myself resonating hard with one or two lines someone wrote, and I'm always so inspired, I want to write.

So there's some of that advice wrapped up in here. But more than that, I think the random or serendipitous potential of an exercise like this is very helpful.

The goal of this exercise is to introduce something into your writing that might not otherwise have been there.

To look at the words someone else wrote and see how they can guide or shape you.

(I get that some of you will reject this advice. Hopefully I've said this enough, but *you should!* Not every piece of advice in this book is for every writer. You should absolutely be rejecting much of it.)

Grab a poem from Plath, Poe, Dickinson, Hughes, Hopkins or someone who's more contemporary. (My favorite living poets are David Whyte and Sherman Alexie if you need somewhere to start.)

Just read the poem first. Let the language drive you.

I have all of David Whyte's poetry books on my shelf and I grab them regularly on rotation. Or I will pull up recordings of poets reading their own poetry or the poetry of others.

I will often grab a line from a poem and throw it into the mouths of my characters (even in internal monologue), just to jumpstart the creativity. (The line doesn't always stay in, by the way. It's just a way to get unstuck.)

Something about the cadence of poetic language always inspires me to write.

For you, it might be song lyrics.

And as always, if you are independently publishing, make sure you have the rights to publish the lines you're using in your books (or that the books are in the public domain). And, as always, watch out for song lyrics and copyrighting. (This is why lines often don't stay in my manuscript when I'm editing.)

But as a way of getting unstuck, I've found it to be incredibly useful.

Resource 6

Do you know your POV character's archetype?

SIMILAR TO OTHER PERSONALITY ALIGNMENT metrics, the archetypes of the hero's journey story can be very helpful for "what should they do next, though" questions.

The most helpful version of this I've found is *The Writer's Journey* by Christopher Vogler. (But if you're not writing a hero's journey story, then this resource will be less helpful. Maybe try *The Heroine's Journey* by Gail Carriger.)

What I like about archetypes is that they are very broad, big-picture collections of character actions that are already aligned to a particular type of story.

When you are writing an epic hero's journey, in order to make all the motivations align, you will need certain characters to appear. They do not have to appear predictably. They do not all have to die or act in the way they have died or acted in the past.

But the reason these patterns exist and are replicated is because they resonate. Sometimes I think we confuse being predictable with being boring, but that's often because as writers, we know how the sausage is made.

I'm just going to suggest re-thinking your relationship to archetypes. If you want a great explanation of why resonant stories are important to fiction, check out *Seven Figure Fiction* by T. Taylor or the work of Dr. Jennifer Lynn Barnes.

And once again, you definitely don't have to use hero's journey archetypes. There are so many different types of storytelling, and each type of storytelling will have its own version of archetypes. They're just helpful patterns that have already outlined emotional resonance.

It's always possible to write an old pattern in a fresh way.

Resource 7

Go to YouTube and type in the job of your main character and the words "how to" and watch a video on their job.

OUR COLLECTIVE DESIRE NOT TO procrastinate often makes us wary of doing things that make us leave the manuscript. But sometimes, when you're drawing a blank, you have to look at what's missing. If you've checked in with other places, and you can't find the answer in your structure or your planning or your character emotions, there might be something *missing* that you can't quantify.

I coached a writer who was very resource driven and he was explaining to me how he needed to understand the job of the character in order to be able to understand them. So he would go to read books on that job (not "for writers" books, just about the job), and read blogs written by someone with that job.

This whole idea fascinated me because it says something about needing to understand the whole-life-context of a particular character. Not just knowing their motivations or their story goals, but about knowing their instincts and what they would do.

Because he was writing space-set science fiction, he mentioned going looking for an earth-based profession like a diplomat as a way to comp a particular diplomatic job on a space station. He was looking for the daily routine, the way the mind worked, the decisions they'd face on a regular basis.

It was a little like studying a working car in order to rebuild a broken car. Looking at the way the engine ran and how everything fired. Using that as a way to look for holes in his character development.

I thought it was brilliant, and ever since then, I've been suggesting the same when authors come to me, uncertain of a character's actions. My favorite stories from authors who've used this have been about the "how to" YouTube videos.

Because YouTube has such a broad cultural appeal, there is a niche for everything. Everyone you could possibly want to study, on this planet, has some kind of YouTube video dedicated to what they do. And the prevalence of "daily vlogs" is high enough, you can get a sense for someone's daily job responsibilities and thoughts by watching their actual life.

This is a card I would reach for when you find yourself really struggling to understand your character, if they have a specific job. The application of this might take some time, and it might feel occasionally like procrastinating, but I always think of this kind of research like a sponge.

If I expect to be able to squeeze water from the sponge, I have to put water in it. The water can't just magically appear. So if I need details about someone's life, I need to go looking for them.

Resource 8

Listen to the "Wish I'd Known Then" podcast on Spotify or iTunes.

THE OWNERS OF THIS PODCAST DO NOT KNOW I've put this into the card deck, or the book, and I hope they'll be okay that I'm suggesting this resource, but I have a very specific reason for suggesting this podcast in particular.

When Jami and Sara first told me what they were planning with their podcast, I will 100% admit to being jealous they came up with this idea before I did. It's a fantastic idea.

Ask a bunch of successful authors what they wish they had known when they started. The content is very focused. Successful authors talking about the lessons they've learned.

It's maybe the best podcast out there for authors right now, and yes, I include my own in that. I love the content here.

Why do I love it so much, specifically for getting unstuck?

So often, when we hear the advice that's meant for us, even at the wrong time, we get an intuitive sense that we should pay attention. And just flipping through the show notes on this podcast, you will see a very wide variety of authors talking about all the mistakes they made.

It's like getting a Master's Degree in publishing without the pesky relocation and fees. The podcast runners are excellent interviewers, and they are both authors themselves, so the podcast is as much about them wanting to know what these authors have learned as it is an effort to help other authors.

Honestly, it's the best podcast for writers I've heard.

It's not tactical. It's not strategic. (Although you will hear both tactics and strategies.) And while the authors are for sure telling their own success stories, it isn't even really about success.

Well. It is about success. But it's not about what they did right.

It's about how they accepted what had gone wrong, learned from it, and kept on moving forward.

Clearly, I am a fan. I think it's worth checking out.

. . .

NOTE: THERE ARE LOTS OF GOOD PODCASTS for authors out there and I haven't heard them all. If you have recommendations for podcasts, we regularly ask for suggestions on the Better-Faster Academy Facebook page. Please feel free to come and leave me a comment if you get this far in the book and you want to tell me about the best podcast I clearly don't know about. I'm nothing if not a resource collector!

Resource 9

When was the last time you read a book, Keri? You might need energy pennies that only reading can provide.

MANY WRITERS BEGAN THEIR WRITING careers as readers. That means reading was a hobby. Even if we wanted to get paid to write, most of us did not start off getting paid to read.

Although, shout-out to the 80s and 90s kids who grew up getting paid in pizzas to read books. I actually read a tweet once where a reader credited Pizza Hut for turning them into book addicts. Thanks, Pizza Hut.

But after we stopped getting paid in pizzas to read and started getting paid in money to write, almost all writers start to feel guilty for reading. Like somehow, reading isn't part of the job of writing.

Every single thing we do, every decision we make, costs us something. If you imagine that we have a certain number of pennies of energy every day, we pay out some of that energy with every decision, every thought, every action, every interaction. Everything is an energy exchange of some kind.

We are rarely aware of this, however, until we're out of energy. Then, we notice. But I'm here to tell you, the energy exchange is minuscule and consistent and costly. (That's why I originally started using the metaphor of pennies. And I apologize to the spoonie community—when I first started coaching, I had never heard of spoons before, and by that time, so much of how I talked about burnout was related to currency, I couldn't change my metaphor. I do apologize for that, because I know there's a whole community of people who use spoons as a metaphor for their energy usage. I use pennies specifically because of the fact that they're tiny currency and most people are unaware of how they spend their currency-pennies, let alone their energy-pennies.)

I use the words "minuscule, consistent, and costly" for very specific reasons.

Miniscule: We are rarely aware, without being made aware, of how much it costs us to perform tasks. When you have an unlimited supply of energy, you tend not to notice how it's spent. And it's important to note that every single decision (should I have coffee or not, should I turn right or left, should I wear the grey or the blue shirt?) costs us, in addition to actual physical exertion costing us. Thoughts cost us pennies. In the most tiny, microscopic ways that we could possibly imagine.

Consistent: For the most part, tasks cost what they cost. It's very rare that a task that's always been easy would suddenly be hard unless something else surrounding the task changed. (And in that case, it wouldn't be the task itself that would be costly, it would be the things surrounding the task.)

Costly: We default to being cost energy. Similarly to how we default to being cost to live. We naturally use resources, just by existing (heat or cooling, light or power, water, space). So there's a cost to us being alive. Someone is paying it. If it isn't me, then it's someone else.

Most of burnout is the ineffective use of energy pennies. But it's not the same as just working too hard. It's almost always the magical addition of something costly to the plate, or the significant change in how much tasks cost me to perform (in a way they didn't before).

And while this isn't necessarily a card about burnout, it is a card about reading, which is one of the primary ways that we can make energy pennies. (Again, this is assuming that you have been a hobby reader—and not all writers will fall into that category.)

There's a reason the IRS considers reading to be part of the work of writing. Yes, some of it is absolutely research. (And maybe, where the government is concerned, it's 100% about the research.) But I'm here to tell you that the upside of reading isn't just about the research. It's also one of the main ways we can refill the energy penny bank, as writers. It's something that can even, at times, be both work and fun.

Being conscious of how much activities cost you can be one of the ways you stave off burnout. If you are doing too many things every day that only cost and never refill, you are going to burn out. We do have banks of pennies that we can spend when we haven't taken pennies in. But those banks are not inexhaustible. We think they are, because we rarely reach the end of them, but they are not unlimited.

So, both as a resource for your potential writing, and as a way to make precious pennies for you to spend on other things, please consider reading a book.

For your mental health.

Resource 10

Go to your favorite course on craft. My favorites are at the Margie Lawson Academy. I always recommend the Dialogue Cues class first.

I'M ABSOLUTELY A FAN OF LEARNING, SO I'M happy to see when authors get interested in taking classes. Learning is growth, so I'm glad for that. But I'm always looking for actual recommendations from students about classes that have *helped* them. Not just the classes that happen across my advertising feed.

So if you're with a group of writers at any point in the future, think about throwing out the question for their favorite classes. And always make sure to ask **why** they liked the class. We're all different and differences matter. One person's favorite class might not have any of the things you need from your learning. It's always important to know that, I think.

So let me talk about why I specifically like Margie's classes.

First, Margie herself is a psychologist. So she's approaching her teaching of writing from an analytical place, and I like that. She's trying to figure out why things work. Why some writing is better than other writing.

She's really a brilliant teacher.

Also, she has a trio of classes that I think every author should at least look at, even if they're not going to take them. Her Empowering Character Emotions, Deep Editing, and Body Language / Dialogue Cues classes are some of the best craft classes I've ever taken (if not the best). She works with a lot of NYT Bestsellers and she's one of the first recommendations in any writer's group I've ever been a part of.

But also, go ask your writer friends. Ask them what classes they've loved, and again, ask why they enjoyed it. What they got out of it. I think it's very important these days to curate the classes you take, and to make sure what you're hoping to get is what others have gotten.

This specific card is about going back to old courses, too, though. It isn't just the new courses we take (because we can sometimes suffer from silver-bullet-seeking, and looking only for the thing that's going to fix our problems once and forever). I also want to see us go back to the courses we've already taken. Many times, we've learned the thing we need to know. We just need to be reminded that we've already learned it.

Go back through the annals of what you've already taken and see what you find. You might find something that will help you in the moment where you're stuck right now.

Resource 11

Turn on Pandora or Spotify and build a playlist for your main character's life.

WHEN I'M WRITING THIS BOOK, WE'RE IN THE end-of-the-year Spotify wrap-up and it's always interesting to see what people listen to. It tells me a lot about them.

(They always think it doesn't, because they think their music tastes are inscrutable. But it tells me a lot about them.)

Because I have always been musical (and I know I'm not alone among writers in being musical), I have always believed what people listen to is indicative of something. So when I build new character profiles, I'm always thinking about what kind of music they like. It gives me a good sense of their vibe.

My Pandora stations are all nothing but character names where I will start with an artist and then start writing. I listen to each subsequent song and vote it up or down based on whether I think the character would like it. So, by the end of the book, I have a pretty heavily curated algorithm of what that person wants to hear when they turn on their radio.

I have a friend who publishes a playlist for each of her characters on her newsletter, and her readers love it. There are all kinds of potential options for this.

Diving deep into the music your character listens to can be a really easy hack to refocus yourself on the story.

Resource 12

Pippa suggests: Go wander around in an art gallery.

ADDITIONAL DOMAIN: ENVIRONMENT

I initially put this piece of advice in environment because it is, ultimately, about a change in environment. But I felt like that domain was full of "you get out what you put in" advice, and I wanted to move it over here and focus on art as a resource.

The colloquialism, "a picture is worth a thousand words," was put into the collective canon for a reason. Because a picture is so big and full of so many details, the eye doesn't stay in only one place.

Yes, it's often drawn to one place at first. But it doesn't stay there. The gaze wanders. Because the gaze wanders, it gives us the opportunity to engage and interact with different parts of the picture.

Think about this for a second.

Get to a computer and go on a big screen. Look for the Millais painting called *Ophelia*. Let your eyes take in the larger painting. Where are you immediately drawn?

What was the first detail that caught your eye? Now, notice your eyes moving around the painting. Focusing on all the small details. If you were looking at this painting live, in, say, London, you might be struck with the texture of it, or the size. You might be arrested by the still-lamenting look on her face. The way she looks in the middle of something.

You might be struck by the light detail on the flowers on her dress.

The longer you look at a painting like this, the more you notice about it. And I find this to be true with almost all art. (I will admit to some artists not being able to hold my attention, so obviously, it's still "to each their own," even with art.) But if you find a painting that really arrests your attention the way *Ophelia* arrests mine, you might get at the heart of this card.

Yes, it's absolutely about immersion into a place where art exists for consumption. And some of it is just about the vibe of the art gallery. But for me, art galleries and museums are specifically places where it's allowable to stop and Narnia into paintings. Where we are expected to take time with the details of art.

I love that.

And of course, it's interesting that Pippa suggested a gallery, and my mind immediately went to museum. Now I think I need to find an art gallery and see if I get the same experience.

Resource 13

Pick up your favorite craft book. Turn past the first few chapters you've already read and go deeper.

NOTICE I ASSUMED YOU HAVEN'T READ THE entire book?

Did you know that Goodreads did a presentation once about book data at a conference and the room was so packed, you could sense the collective anticipation. (This was after they were purchased by Amazon, so I think one of the selling points was that they might have some of that Kindle data. To be fair, I don't know whether or not they did have Kindle data, but the findings of their database were pretty incredible.)

One of the things I remember the most from that workshop was their discussion of how many books were *finished*.

More than 80% of books on Goodreads were never read past the 50% mark. But of the books where readers consistently read past 50%, they almost always read 100%.

I'm making a huge general assumption here about you and your craft book reading. And maybe I'm wrong. Maybe you're in that 20% of people who are finishing all their books. But let me just assume that you trend the way most people I know trend.

Go read one of the later chapters in your craft books. Maybe that one your friends really liked but you couldn't get into. Maybe that one everyone recommends. Maybe your favorite that you honestly haven't read all the way through.

In general, I'm a huge fan of going back and re-reading. We often miss so much when we read the first time. Also, re-presenting data to ourselves is a way of re-experiencing the information anew.

Even if you've never re-read a craft book in your life, do me the favor of going back. Pick one you thought was great. Re-read a chapter. (It doesn't have to be the first one.)

See what happens when you re-experience data.

(You might do the same for your old favorite workshops, although I think we already talked about that. Maybe just go through your old notes. Refresh your memory.)

We have a common colloquial phrase in English called "outside the box" which inherently assumes that being "in the box" is a bad thing, and being "outside the box" is a good thing. Inside the box is constraint and predictability, and we want to value thinking that breaks the pattern we have in the box.

A good portion of us are comfortable with things inside the box, so we don't often think about how to disrupt our patterns. In fact, if you are both comfortable and happy inside the box, we might even view people who predictably disrupt as annoyances.

When you don't like change, disruption is not your friend.

Here's what I can promise in this domain:

I'm trying only to disrupt the things that I think might help us to gain the benefit of a different perspective. I chose the cards in this domain very specifically, because I have seen these disruptions present a specific kind of help to authors. I'll explain why each of these have been helpful to others.

(And of course, those of you who are already fans of disruptions are thinking, *why are we coddling these people, Becca?* I get that. When you are naturally a fan of disrupting patterns, this domain will be more interesting to you. But we do sometimes have to convince others the disruption is worthwhile.)

If you've ever seen the idea diffusion curve, you know why. More than 80% of the population actively resists pattern change—in fact, they resist it so much because when you're in the right pattern, it's really helpful to not have to think too much about whether or not you're doing things the right way.

But sometimes, the patterns are unhelpful.

This domain is for those times when the patterns are unhelpful, or when we won't be able to get out of the stuck rut until we drastically change our thinking.

Surprise will do that.

How to Use These Surprises

If you are used to disrupting your own writing, you might not need this section. But if you are not used to it, I'm going to encourage you to always make a copy of the manuscript and save the "undisrupted" version in case you need to go back to it.

What I typically do when I have to disrupt my manuscript is I will copy the previous chapter into the new document (or I'll copy in a few chapters if I'm in the middle of a book) and start a completely new document that only has the "new" writing in it.

Somehow, that tricks my intuitive brain into remembering that this is an experiment.

I have clients who have tried the "just open a brand new manuscript" thing, and it's worked for them. So you might be a brand-new-manuscript person, as well.

One way or the other, though, I would always put the disrupted manuscript in a separate place from the old manuscript. If you're using a program like Scrivener, you have the option of just starting a new chapter and knowing that if you don't touch the chapters behind, you're not really changing anything. But it's important to note that it's not uncommon for these disruptions to need tossing (even if they help you realize what needed to happen in the original manuscript).

Sometimes, that's their entire purpose. Just to give you a chance to write something else that you eventually toss when your brain works out what *should* have happened.

Surprise 1

Chris suggests, "Change your manuscript to a ridiculous comic font."

PEOPLE RARELY BELIEVE ME THAT THIS WILL work. And of course, because I'm formatting in Vellum, I can't show you just how different a sentence would look in contrast. But go try it for yourself. Try just changing one sentence first and see how that goes.

What we're looking for in this domain is "thinking different" about what's in the manuscript currently.

This tactic is especially helpful when you're in editing mode and can't see the forest for the trees anymore. That little change in how you perceive the story can really help.

(That's also, on a side note, why talking about the story can help. When you have to change the medium, you often change the perspective.)

Surprise 2

Throw an obstacle in the character's path that makes them unable to get what they want right now.

THIS OBSTACLE NEEDS TO COME OUT OF nowhere. Predictable obstacles aren't going to disrupt. And it has to be right now. Right where you're stuck. Don't write your way into it. Interrupt whatever was happening in the scene.

You might have a character pop up to tell your protagonist the person they seek is dead.

You might give them a flat tire or make their horse run off, or otherwise impede the method of transportation they're using.

You might have their weaponry malfunction or have someone steal or disarm them of their weapon.

You might send in weather that completely befuddles their trajectory and forces them to interact with people you hadn't planned.

You might empty their house of condoms.

You might set fire to their bakery or to their police station or to their home or place of business.

Notice if you feel "disrupted" by this advice. And even if you have to make a copy of your manuscript to see where this might go, just try doing something disruptive.

I watched a masterful oral storyteller try to keep a group of children entertained for a long time once. We were in an environment where we had no access to the internet, and the activity we'd planned next fell through, and we suddenly had a bunch of time to kill.

We'll call the storyteller Steve.

Once we realized the next activity was unreachable, Steve gathered all the kids into a circle and said, "I'm going to tell you a story."

I expected him to do something we'd all heard before, or tell a plot from a movie or something, but he started into an original story.

One of the most interesting parts about watching Steve do this was how carefully he watched that group of kids. We were all worried that they would start complaining and misbehaving, but Steve was prepared with his disruptive mind.

His little trio of intrepid adventurers would head in one direction, and as soon as he noticed the kids were losing their interest, he would throw in an obstacle. It caught their attention. It wasn't what they had expected.

So Steve would continue along that path until *bam!* A dragon suddenly appeared when the trio thought they were well on their way. And then they'd have to fight the dragon, but *bam!* One of them was injured and they had to take that person to a mentor for help. But then *bam!* The mentor turned out to be one of the villain's henchmen.

He kept that audience of kids engaged by disrupting their expectations. As much as he could, he tried to watch the whole group, and make sure, as soon as their attention wandered, *bam!* Disruption.

I can't remember the whole story because once the mentor turned into a henchman, I had to go figure out our next activity, so I was only partly paying attention. But Steve managed to keep that group of kids engaged for almost thirty minutes, just by throwing obstacle after obstacle in the characters' paths.

As writers, we often underestimate the value of a good obstacle. Especially in the middle of the book, where the threads are starting to play out.

I'm just saying.

Obstacles are helpful. If your protagonists are getting what they want all the time... they need an obstacle anyway. Give them a good one.

Surprise 3

Open your manuscript and, wherever your cursor is, type one of the following sentences:

And then everything changed.

And then the murders began.

And then she saw someone she never thought she'd see again.

And then the dragons came.

And then she heard a loud pop behind her.

Obviously, change the gender if you're not writing in the female POV, but the rest of the sentence should stay the same.

The goal here is to introduce something that will facilitate a change, and to plan the catalyst, but to give you an opportunity to have some control over where you go next.

And yes, you can still use *dragons* in a contemporary manuscript. This might refer to a group of high-powered investors (think *sharks*) or a group of bullies or a sports team. But dragons will still work.

The possibilities are endless here. And it might even be beneficial to go looking for sentences like this as you're reading. Collect sentences that do this shift in action with one phrase.

You don't have to keep the exact wording if you'd rather not. But using these action shifts randomly can be helpful.

(I'm still hoping to read a book someday where I see the sentence "and then the murders began" so I can know someone else read that meme. And I can never remember where I saw that meme, but maybe I've seen it so many times now, it's become urban legend.)

Go into your manuscript and write one of those sentences wherever your cursor is located. Go on! Type away.

Surprise 4

Give your character a secret sibling. Someone they didn't even know about.

AND YES, EVEN IF YOU'RE WRITING contemporary, and even if they had two loving parents. The person could be pretending to be their sibling for some reason.

I'm a big fan of secret siblings, as you will no doubt know if you read any of my books. And now that my sister has done the 23andMe thing, I'm fairly certain I have no secret siblings. So it's not from personal experience. There's just something really interesting about how much your life would have to change orientation if you discovered a secret of that magnitude.

But the addition of a sibling they didn't know about is meant to disrupt their feelings about their family and past. Do I really know my family the way I thought?

I understand if you want to push back against this one. Just remember, start a new manuscript so you don't mess up the current one if this doesn't end up staying.

And it's ok if it doesn't stay. I'm just trying to have a moment of disruption to their sense of self to see what comes up.

Sometimes, we find our relationships are so strong, it wouldn't impact the way we feel about anyone. And sometimes, it will.

I think it's important to at least provide the character the opportunity to see if anything would change.

Surprise 5

Kill someone.
(A character, Lexi... kill a character.)

DON'T KILL ANYONE IN REAL LIFE, OBVIOUSLY. That should go without saying, but nothing is certain in this world anymore.

I'm also going to make an argument for killing someone you think you can't kill. (If you're in a romance, no, I don't mean one of the main characters who are involved in the love story... although, if it's a love triangle...)

Also, I will never get over the TikTok that said it's not a love triangle unless the two love interests are also potentially interested in each other. Otherwise, it's a Love V. Blew my mind. Thanks, TikTok.

Ok, back to killing people.

The reason I'm trying to make an argument to kill someone you think you need… the disruption. Kill the sidekick. Kill the person the main character is seeking. Kill the person who was supposed to give them this vital bit of information they've been chasing.

Once again, this is about the character not getting what they want and forcing them to find other ways to get the thing.

And of course, if you're Nick Sparks, you can go ahead and kill a love interest. We expect it from you at this point, buddy.

Again, I hate to argue in favor of murder. But I am a mystery writer, so maybe I don't.

The old mystery writer adage is, "when in doubt, drop a body." So just for a second, be a mystery writer.

Surprise 6

What if you erased the entire chapter you're currently working on and started over?

You can save it somewhere if you need to. But just try this. See what would happen if you completely erased a chapter (and didn't refer back to it as you wrote the new version).

This is something I routinely suggest when people are very stuck. (Like nothing they've worked so far will help them.) It's so common for us to have made mistakes in the plot trajectory directly behind us when we get stuck, and sometimes, erasing can be just the thing to remind us of what we did.

I understand the reluctance to do this. And if it makes you more stuck when you do it, abandon quickly and go back to the other chapter. But at least consider trying it out.

Just for the disruption of thinking alone.

Surprise 7

Give your character a secret past. Something they have never told anyone.

MANY OF US DO THIS FORM OF DISRUPTION without realizing they've disrupted the character's inner life. But also, if *you* know what the secret is, then that's not the kind of secret I mean.

I mean something that even you don't know right now. You may invent it as you go along, or you may have to go back in and seed the secret in other places. But if you really want to disrupt, give your character a secret even you don't know.

Again, make a separate copy of the manuscript, and then see how it goes. I would say *report back*, but we're not coaching. Still, I like to know the results of this when I coach for two reasons:

1. If it significantly changes the plot, sometimes the writer will need to check in about whether they want to keep going down this road or not.

2. If it doesn't change anything, then it didn't do the disruption it needed to do, and we have to pull another card, in a manner of speaking.

But sometimes, this kind of secrecy folds its way into the story so easily, there's a likelihood you were already planning for this kind of secret to exist. And then it hasn't disrupted.

So we need to disrupt in another way.

Surprise 8

Give your character a tool. Something they have to hold in their hands that they didn't have before.

THIS NEEDS TO BE SOMETHING YOU HADN'T previously written about. (You can always go back in and seed it later if you need to.) It's a surprise to them, and to the reader.

In this case, it needs to be a surprise to you, too.

The tool can be helpful for the situation they're in, but it could also be a tool they don't necessarily need. (Someone hands them a hammer in the middle of a board meeting. Someone gives them a phone that isn't theirs. They pick up a saw from off the ground. They find an axe among their lover's things.)

But it doesn't have to be a construction style tool. There are lots of other tools. Computers, typewriters, pens, glasses, sponges. So many tools. So little time.

In fact, if there is a tool randomizer somewhere, try that. Try someone giving you a random suggestion in a Facebook group or a Discord channel.

The only rules are: it needs to be something the character should use and hold in their hands. Whether they use the tool or not is up to you. But put it in their hands.

Surprise 9

What if you skipped a month in the scene you're about to write? A year? Ten years?

IN THE *Six Categories of Stuck* CHAPTER, I TALKED about the client who had been asked to skip ten years from the scene in their book, and my creative friend (who is a natural disruptor) who asked the question.

The glitch from that first disruption was so immediate and so visible, I still remember it. Like, *no, I can't do that in this genre.*

And the whole point of disruption is to think outside the box. So if you find yourself not pushing back at skipping a month, but pushing back at a year or ten years, then write the one you pushed back on. Not the one you would easily have been able to do.

Again, the point of disruption is to do the thing that pushes us out of our comfort zone. Not the thing we would easily have done on our own. That's not disruptive. That's expected.

Write the disrupted version. Or at least let your brain go there.

Surprise 10

That thing your character is about to do... what if they did the exact opposite thing? Make them do it and see what happens.

THIS IS ONE WHERE I COMMONLY GET pushback when I bring it up in coaching. I hear, "but they have to pick up the letter—it has the clue in it," or some version of that. The thing the author has planned for the character to do is advancing the plot.

Right, Janice, I get that.

But could you find a way for the plot to advance if they do the exact opposite thing?

A client tried this once, where the detective was supposed to grab their gun and run out of the house to chase down a lead and I asked the writer what would happen if their police officer didn't grab a gun.

The client glitched. "She has to grab the gun."

"But what if she didn't?"

Glitch. "No. She has to. She's a detective. She wouldn't chase down a subject without her gun."

"But what if she did?"

What we realized (after another few minutes of this back and forth) was that something would have to change about the detective's current mental state in order to facilitate her not grabbing her gun. The writer had to give her a motivation to not grab the weapon.

Since they'd tried to write this particular scene several times and kept glitching when the detective grabbed her gun and ran out of the house, I suggested this "do the opposite" advice.

(Note: that's often exactly when this needs to happen. When you keep glitching in the same place, over and over.)

The detective's motivation turned out to be something that was generally lacking in the story and the writer hadn't seen the lack before. They added another character, who ended up being crucial to the story.

I have no doubt they would have figured out the lack of motivation at some point on their own. But they were stuck, and they needed some kind of disruption that would make the story present itself in their subconscious.

This is a lesson about the "do the opposite thing" advice, as well. We can't just do the opposite thing, sometimes. We often have to change other details in the story in order to make that work.

In this case, the question becomes, "what has to change in order to make that opposite action happen?"

Then write the change.

Surprise 11

Go watch a movie, Maya. Extra points if it reminds you of your book. I'll wait.

BECAUSE I'VE SPOKEN ELSEWHERE ABOUT THE judgments we place on ourselves for enjoying parts of the process, I won't belabor this.

Nope. Nevermind.

We're belaboring.

Just because you enjoy something doesn't mean it isn't still work. And there may even be many parts of the process of creating *entertainment* (which is the category books fall into) that will be entertaining.

But.

I did say "movie" and not "tv show" for a reason. (Sometimes, a TV show is the thing, of course, and sometimes it's the only activity that will really work to get you unstuck. But TV shows can be a bit dangerous.) Most of us who have streaming services know the inescapable lure of "one more episode."

So if you decide that a TV show will be your un-stuck of choice, and not a movie, make sure you create a catalyst for yourself to go back to the book.

Maybe you open the manuscript after every episode.

At the very least, I would get up off the couch/floor/chair and walk around after each episode. Hit pause and move around.

Whenever we can, we do want to disrupt stasis.

But I'm a huge fan of the movie because it has a discrete beginning and end. Many of us need this immersion in a visual medium or story in order to get through some part of the story that's sticking us. Whatever it takes.

Surprise 12

Ask a friend for a word to use in your next sentence.

MY VERY FIRST WRITING GROUP USED TO DO this exercise called the Poetry of Three Things where we would select three people to give a word. It had to be selected ahead of time, and we would often try to be as random as possible.

It could be a verb, a noun, or an adjective, but it could only be one word. (And also, it could be a proper noun, though we rarely did this in practice.)

The three people would put their words in the center of the table and someone else would read them out.

Once all three words were selected, we would each have to write a poem or a piece of short fiction that used all three of those words.

At the end of the exercise, we would each read aloud what we'd written, and it was fairly amazing how different everyone's work would be. We never even had a sniff of similarity between each person's writing.

I went through a period in my twenties where I used to write Poetry of Three Things every day. (I have files and files of them saved. Short fiction or poems.) I'd go to word randomizers or ask friends to give me words, and it helped me to practice the art of incorporating random things into my work.

Honestly, I think this is one of the best skills I've acquired as a writer because it helped me learn flexibility within my own expectations. I also learned to appreciate serendipity. (Although if you know me, you know I already had a healthy appreciation for that, from birth, and this probably just played on that capacity I already had.) But I'm a huge fan of the surprise of random words.

It makes you think differently about your expectations.

Just try it with one of the following words. Open your manuscript and, in the next sentence or paragraph, use one of these:

Baguette

Penny

Bow

Magenta

Hinge

Icing

Thorough

Arrow

Virile

Senile

Wavy

Brusque

Nightingale

Souffle

Tire Iron (ok, that was two words, but you get it...)

May the serendipity of the randomizer be ever in your favor. And honestly, it might be worth doing something like the Poetry of Three Things (although, again, it can be short fiction, it was just nice to use P3T as an acronym) on a regular basis.

Exercise your creative muscles in a way that doesn't have to be about using the words in a product.

So many of us need to learn how to do things we don't monetize. Our brains are tired from all the monetizing. How about just finding the joy in the writing for the sake of the writing?

Sigh. I know, I know.

But just consider it.

Surprise 13

Roll dice.
Go to that book (from the left) on your bookshelf.
Roll dice again.
Go to that page.
Roll again.
Count the words from the top of the page and use
that word in your next sentence.

ANOTHER RANDOM-WORD-GENERATOR. PLUS, it introduces the luck of the dice roll, which I also like a lot.

In fact, you could very easily turn your writing into a sort of D&D roll, where you have decided what the numbers on the dice mean. We have a graphic like this that we made for our Patreon community. If you would like it, and you've made it this far into the book, when you get to the "What's Next" page, we'll give you a link to download that.

No, it's not a lead magnet to our mailing list. There will be a separate place to sign up for that if you want to. This is just a tool you can use if you like dice rolls and you're interested in using the dice more often in your writing.

I'm sure LitRPG authors are already doing this all the time. But since our audience includes writers who might not already know D&D, I find myself wanting to make sure... do you have 20-sided dice? If not, and you decide to download the tool, make sure you do. There are 20 options.

But beyond that tool, try this dice roll tactic for yourself. The roll is a great randomizer. I find that the embracing of random actions and tactics will help in the disruption process.

Randomness disrupts regular life all the time. Why not fiction?

This is something I'd love to hear about if you do it. If you've made it this far in the book, there's a good chance you are interested in connecting, so make sure you find us on Facebook or Instagram or TikTok and let me know how this worked for you.

In Closing

THE GOAL OF THIS BOOK WAS TO PROVIDE A comprehensive tool to deal with manuscript and process stuck-ness in a way that can be customized to you and to your process.

I feel good about the work we've done here. And if you are interested in customizing your own process, now you have the "why" behind why any individual piece of advice might work. I would hope, additionally, you can extrapolate the "why" of other pieces of advice from the basic structure. I tried to be as comprehensive as I can.

Hopefully you were taking notes for yourself as you were reading, or you will be able to come back to this book anytime.

If you need additional help, we do a live free public coaching session every month, and if you follow our

Facebook page at The Better-Faster Academy, you'll be able to find our next one.

Also, there are several episodes of the QuitCast (our YouTube channel) that talk about different facets of stuck-ness, including a recent episode on the fear of the blank page. I hope you will avail yourselves of all these free resources we provide.

Now that you're finished the book, and you know where you can find us, here's the hope I have:

You have a list of things you can quickly do when you're stuck.

So many of us circle around, not knowing what to do, and really, we're in decision fatigue, when we can't make progress on the manuscript. I hope to give you the ability to move forward as quickly as possible with some things to try.

If you find this tool helpful, please do share it with your writing friends. My hope is, if the tool is helpful, people will share it, and if it isn't, then it'll stay on Amazon and not sell and we'll work on something else that will be more helpful.

But I want writers to be able to write more easily and more effectively (whether they write consistently or not). When we sit down to write, I'd like to help us get to the writing. The creating.

That's always the thing I hope with any of our products, classes, or coaching. I would hope they help writers get to the creating more and better-faster (that great hybrid place of flow).

Thank you so much for spending this time with me. I hope this tool will be something you reach for, in the years to come.

Happy writing.

<3 Becca <3

———

THANK YOU FOR READING *The Author Stuck List*!

I invite you to join the Better-Faster Newsletter to get my Stuck List Roll Tables.

These roll tables are meant to help get you unstuck when you need a little serendipity in your novel.

betterfasteracademy.com/newsletter-stucklist-book

Using the Card Deck As a Companion

IN CASE YOU ARE INTERESTED IN USING THE cards along with this, we will be running regular Kickstarters for other tools to help writers. Each time we run a Kickstarter, we will include these cards as an available add-on.

There is a companion workbook that comes as a download. All of the information from both the card deck and the workbook are contained in this book, though. So there's no need to purchase them out of FOMO. Only purchase the cards if you genuinely will use the physical deck in a way you won't use this book.

Read a short excerpt below

CHAPTER ONE
The Bad News

Some of you picked up this book because, when you saw the title, you thought, "Do I need to quit writing?"

Some of you are here to see the dumpster fire for yourself. You also watch car accident videos on YouTube or the *Real Housewives* of something or other. I see you.

Or you're just curious. *Who is this chick and why does she think I need to quit something?*

And a few of you picked it up because you want ammunition to roast me for having the gall to tell anyone what to do. Go on. I'll wait.

But most of you are wondering what (if anything) you need to quit, and you're curious about what's inside this book.

So let me get the bad news out of the way.

Yes. Some people do need to quit writing. But chances are good, none of those people will ever read these pages.

If, by some miracle, you are considering quitting, and this book confirms that for you, please know this: it is okay to quit if that's what's best for you. Too many people will try to force you to keep going, despite your own feelings, despite potential burnout, despite a crowded market, despite the thousands of dollars you're throwing into your books and not making the money back yet... despite maybe even your own desire to be done.

So... yes, some of us do need to quit writing.

I hope that's not why you're here. You may have wondered if you need to quit, but deep down, you know that's not the problem. The problem lies elsewhere—you're just not sure where it is. This book can help to uncover that problem.

More likely than not, you're here to learn. If that's your goal, then you will likely fulfill it.

On one hand, I do want some of us to quit writing, for our own good. On the other hand, I also hope that the instruction to quit will create a rebellion deep in your soul if that's not your path—a rebellion that gives me the proverbial finger and says you're going your own way. I would love that. However the fire stokes.

But there are some things that we all need to quit doing, especially if we don't quit writing. So if you've been looking for confirmation that it's time for you to stop, then read this book first. Consider giving up the behaviors that are the source of your stress.

Then, if you still feel the urge, dear writer, you need to quit.

WHY BAD NEWS?

I've been coaching for almost thirteen years (far past the 10,000-hour mark)—thousands of people in corporate, non-profit, and individual settings, nearly two thousand of whom are writers. For the last three years, specifically, I have been teaching a class called *Write Better-Faster* which is a success alignment course designed for fiction writers, but it attracts creatives of all kinds.[1]

In every class I teach, there's one lecture, fairly close to the beginning, where I give you the bad news. Because there's always bad news. Any class or book that doesn't give you the bad news is a ridiculous waste of your time because when bad things happen (and they **will**), you're unprepared for the pushback and it makes you question the entire premise of the class.

My bad news is: There is no silver bullet.

Not only do silver bullets not exist (one shot of ammunition that takes down the monster is literally *fiction*), but more specifically, this book is not a silver bullet. It's not a magic pill. There's no piece of information you're ever going to read that will cure your problems forever. I've coached thousands of people in my career, and let me tell you, each one of them who underwent transformation had to **do the work** to get to the better place.

We're all writers here... think of the character arc. You write a book with a character in one place in the beginning, and you want them to be in a *transformed* place by the end. What happens in the middle?

STORMS.

Trials, tribulation, conflict. And a lot of hard work.

Eventually, they have to face their shadow and decide to be the best version of themself.

You write these stories of transformation all day long, every day, some of you, and yet you still expect your own journey of transformation to be **easy**.

Don't be stupid.

I'm sorry to be harsh here, but stories are resonant because they *feel* true, in their core. Black moments are part of life. The bad news is, nothing will ever truly transform you that won't be a crucible.

It's going to be hard. It's probably gonna suck a lot. Stop expecting things to be easy. That's an unrealistic expectation that will never serve you. It will only handicap you.

Let's release it now, before you start this book. Because if you're looking for a silver bullet, you're gonna be disappointed every time you end a class, finish a session, or close a book. This happens to you all the time, doesn't it?

You take a class, you have an epiphany. You know you need to do the work, so you make lists and plans and you get ready to change. And then that enthusiasm wears off. So you go looking for another book or class or coach.

There's a pattern here.

It's not that you haven't found the "magic pill" **yet**. It's that the magic pill **doesn't exist**. I wish I had better news, but I don't. I've been to Mordor and back, and trust me, Sauron is real, and he's pissed.

And you have to take the ring, Frodo. No eagle shortcuts. No spells. You have to walk the path. Take a buddy, sure, but you can't say no to this journey, Katniss. It's the only way.

If you don't do the work, the change won't stick.

In the story of you, the silver bullet is the temptation. Not the resolution. You're not going to learn something that will instantly transform you. You may learn something that catalyzes action, but if you don't keep that action up, you're never going to reap long-term rewards.

C.S. Lewis wrote an incredible story about transformation that I use often to invite people into this journey. Eustace Scrubb, in *The Voyage of the Dawn Treader*, was prickly, mean, and self-centered. One night, when he was feeling especially sorry for himself, he laid down in a dragon's lair and woke up as a dragon—the external representation of his internal state of being.

When Eustace asks Aslan (the all-powerful lion) to change him from a dragon back into a boy, he gets instructions to go to a pool on the island and peel off his dragon skin. It's painful, and he does it, but when he looks at himself in the pool, he's still a dragon.

So he tries again. Again, it hurts, but he holds back from the real pain, finishes peeling, and when he looks into the pool, he still sees a dragon.

This time, Aslan does the peeling. He digs deep. All the way to the bone. It is the most painful thing Eustace can imagine—something he never would have chosen for himself—and it seems to last forever, but when it's done, there's Eustace in the flesh, looking back from the pool.

This resonates so much because we never want pain for ourselves. We actively push against it when life offers it to us. But the pain is exactly what we need. When we transform into our best self, it *should* be hard. If it wasn't, we'd still be a dragon.

In the case of this metaphor, and as it relates to writers, Becca, what is "a dragon"? What am I transforming out of and into?

I know this is a cop-out answer, but it's different for every person. And I mean that both from a theoretical standpoint (because we're all SO different) and a practical standpoint (I've observed, in thousands of people, there's no one answer). I do what I do (coaching writing systems and transformation processes) because most of us don't understand just how different we are, let alone how much those differences impact everything about us.

But each of the following "quit" chapters is about a particular pattern of transformation I've coached people through. Quitting something is a transformation process because you have to turn into a person who *doesn't do the thing* you're subconsciously programmed to do.

If there was "one" guiding principle for transformation that works, it would be: alignment[2]. Alignment is symmetry between your self and your systems. Between your purpose, your personality, your platform, your capacity, and your goals.

It's not easy, but it's worth it.

Remember the transformational character arc? Full of black moments and low points. And at each of those points, your character has a choice. Go back to life as it is (and stay untransformed—keep peeling off your own skin) or face the storm and let that storm change you.

Let's face your storm together.

THE REAL BAD NEWS

In my day job, I am a success coach. I work primarily with creatives (novelists, screenwriters, picture book writers, illustrators, directors, producers, artists, nonfiction writers, and editors). I've coached almost two thousand creatives (mostly writers of some kind) as of this book's publication. But outside of that work, I've been coaching success alignment and organizational leadership for thirteen years, so I've seen thousands of people and been privy to their thoughts and motivations, and I've learned something important from all that experience.

There's the bad news that I give people (no magic pill), and then the real bad news (the truth underneath that assertion). The real bad news is that most of us won't do the work. We are only looking for the silver bullet, so when we don't find it, we move on. Based on my experience in coaching (as well as knowing other coaches and reading literature on this phenomenon), most people who attempt adult behavioral change don't assimilate it. So the true bad news is that most of you reading this won't do the work.

I wish that you would.

Some of the resistance is the work itself: the fact that it takes time and doesn't happen fast enough; the fact that it isn't fun. Some pushback is the inertia that will eventually reject big change to your life system. Whatever happens, you probably won't be prepared for it, and it will break your resolve. That's just statistics (and my experience) talking.

My hope is that you would prove me wrong.

THE HAPPY NEWS

Now that the bad news and the really bad news are out of the way, let's get to the happy news.

If you do the work, if you quit the things, you will be on the path toward alignment and transformation. It won't be easy—like the hero's journey is ever easy, y'all? Nope.

Only you can make the choice to do this. But that's fantastic news, because you have agency in this story. You are your own main character. You get to make your choices. You can choose to leave behind the weight of baggage that's dragging you down. I've seen people do it. I know it's possible.

I hope this book will inspire you to quit all the things.

WHAT THIS BOOK IS NOT

I've already said, this isn't a silver bullet or a magic pill. It is also not a substitute for therapy. If you need legitimate psychological help, please don't pass that up. Don't substitute coaching for therapy. I am not a therapist. I don't even play one on TV. I do have education, a Master's degree in Transformational Leadership no less, and I have a lot of experience in success coaching, but never substitute something else for therapy when you need it.

This book is also not an excuse to procrastinate whatever is stalling in your manuscript right now. So if you're here procrastinating, that hard spot in the book isn't gonna go away. Get back to the manuscript. Read this book after you write your words. Go.

This book is not meant to substitute for coaching, either. If you really do need someone to sit with you and lay out an individualized success plan, there are plenty of success coaches out there. I use a writing coach. More than one. Unlike therapy, which focuses on what's wrong with you, coaching focuses on what's right, where you have potential, and where you could be successful.

So, if you need a coach, find one. Most of you are here because you're looking for help. Don't settle for someone else's system when you could get assistance finding your own. (More on that later.)

This book is also not The Be-All and End-All of Creative Instruction. It's the product of a lot of learning and synthesis of great writers and thinkers, and the product of thousands of hours of watching patterns and seeing where writers struggle and where they don't. That is my gift. I've been able to sit with some amazing and talented people—six and seven figure authors, mid-listers, major award winners, and newbies alike—and they've shared deeply with me. After enough pattern watching, I see the trends.

It's time to quit some stuff, people.

WHAT THIS BOOK IS

This book is part homage to all the great writers that I've coached or been coached by. It's part tough love. It's part soft spot to land. This book is basically my coaching philosophy on paper. It's a collection of some of the wisdom I've gathered from my experience coaching writers.

If there's one thing I've noticed (both through my work with CliftonStrengths® and in my broad coaching career), it's that people pattern in really consistent ways. Even those of you who think you're so unique, nothing could ever predict your behavior... that's a pattern.

The good news about the fact that human behavior patterns consistently is that if you look at those patterns, you can find comfort in them. And find answers.

My hope for this book is that, by pointing out the patterns in how brains can work, I will give you some tools to look at your own brain. This is something we do in my *Write Better-Faster* class in more depth, but you can do it just fine without my class. Look at how your brain patterns, and then seek out recommendations for writing systems based on those patterns. Not because the patterns are magic, but because when you have a specific road block, what matters most is how you process the road block, how you are motivated, and how you could be successful.

I want this book to be your catalyst to action. I hope you will read it and be inspired to tackle your road blocks. To quit what you need to quit, keep what you need to keep, and question every premise.

End of Sample
To continue reading, be sure to pick up *Dear Writer, You Need to Quit* at your favorite retailer.

About the Author

Becca Syme holds a master's degree in transformational leadership and has been a success coach (primarily utilizing the Gallup Strengthsfinder®) for over fifteen years. She's coached over 5,000 individual authors and creatives through her *Write Better-Faster* and *Strengths for Writers* classes & coaching cohorts: six- and seven-figure authors, major award winners, midlisters, and new authors alike. Becca is the host of the YouTube QuitCast for Writers channel and a mystery author.

betterfasteracademy.com

Also by Becca Syme

QuitBooks for Writers

Dear Writer, You Need to Quit

Dear Writer, Are You In Burnout?

Dear Writer, You're Doing It Wrong

Dear Writer, Are You In Writer's Block?

Dear Writer, You're Doing It Right

Dear Writer, Are You Intuitive?

————

Better-Faster Author Success

The Author Stuck List

Acknowledgments

I'M JUST GONNA BE REAL HONEST HERE AND thank Panera Bread for having a restaurant near my house. Because after the burnout I've been through this year, I'm not sure I would have been able to write if I hadn't had another office location to go to.

I practice what I preach when it comes to being stuck— sometimes I really need the environment to be different, and I've stopped being frustrated with this and just learned to deal with it.

Thank God for the Unlimited Sip Club.

I'm so grateful to Zoe, who edited this book for me, and who has been a long time BFA fan, so she also made sure to tell me that she enjoyed reading it. I always hope reading my stuff isn't a chore.

Thank you to all my friends who listen to me talk about being under deadline and then have to hear me whine when the deadline approaches and I still haven't started. You are all saints. You know who you are.

This book wouldn't exist without the Kickstarter backers. I want to first thank those who contributed advice to the book: Alexis Calder, AM Roark, Chris Cooper, and Pippa Grant. And then, to everyone who allowed me to use their first names so I wasn't just getting mad at George all the time: Aidy Award, Ali Cross, Gina Rinderle, Jen Lassalle, Jillian Liota, Keri Stevens, Lexi Haughton, Lyra Parish, Maya Hughes, Stacy Claflin. Special thanks to these Kickstarter backers: Hannah Jane, Emme G., Brighton W., Luisa PA, Mia Harlan, Claudia B., Paula, Nita S., Golden Angel, Leilani A., Alexis "A.M." Roark, Tracy Cembor, Cassidy T., Savannah F., Marianne H., Amy O., Leslie, Jayne Rylon, Sally Henson, Ed D., Sienna Snow, Gillian SK, L Christensen, Staci M., Martha C., Enid, Pippa Grant, and Alexis Calder.

The entire BFA staff... You know how important you are to me and to the work we do here. Thank you.

To all the writers I've coached and all the students who have come through the BFA classes: thank you.

To everyone on my Patreon: y'all are the literal best. I'm so grateful to be part of this community of writers.

To the Kickstarter backers who showed an interest in this, even before it was a real thing: Thank you so much for making me feel like there's support for this book.

To God and to my family, I am eternally grateful.

And to you, dear reader—dear writer—I wish you all the un-sticking from all your future manuscripts. Forever.

<3 Becca <3

Notes

3. The Six Categories of Stuck

1. Question the premise is a coaching tool I developed to help writers question advice given them. No advice works for everyone (no writing advice you have ever heard is 100% applicable, from "don't edit as you go" to "writers write." I go into this in more depth in my other books, and on my YouTube Channel (The QuitCast for Authors) so I likely won't delve as deeply into the QTP method in this book. But know, all writing advice is relative. All. I have receipts.

2. While "you can't edit a blank page" has been passed around the annals of writing advice for years, we never stop to question whether or not it's actually true. In fact, there is a whole swath of writing brains who are wired to edit in their heads. This means, before they ever set words down on the page, they are editing that page. In their head. They are, in point of fact, editing blank pages ALL THE TIME.

   So while I get the heart behind this (and I also stipulate that not everyone can edit a blank page), we really need to be careful about how we make assumptions about the writing processes of other writers.

   Plenty of writers edit blank pages before they write them, and trying to vomit out words, for those writers, ruins their natural process.

4. Using This Book

1. We have a printable version of this workbook available under the "New To Us?" Tab at http://betterfasteracademy.com if you want it. But you don't need the workbook printed pages to complete this task.

Clarity 7

1. The class is called "Digging Deep Into the Edits System" and it's at the Margie Lawson Academy. I'm not getting any kickbacks from any of these authors or content creators to mention their stuff. I mention helpful tools because I'm also a writer and I've found tools that have helped me. But I always want to caveat with, not all tools work for everyone. So make sure you're looking for help with the specific problem the classes or books solve before you go and buy them.

   Or, of course, those of us who are heavy into learning will go try out all the things, and I will bless you on your way. Although I always like to say, let's make sure to open the manuscript as well. (I know.)

Emotion 5

1. AUTHOR'S NOTE: I want to take a moment to talk about the impact of long term disability and chronic illness on writing. First, you should know that many writers have long term disability and chronic illness, and if you have a disability or an illness, that doesn't preclude you from being a writer, so I hope I'm speaking about tiredness in a way that can be helpful to anyone.

   When we coach people, we believe them when they say, "yes I can" or "no I can't," when we give any level of advice, and that extends to every piece of advice. If there's ever anything I say that doesn't take into account something that's different for you than it is for the advice I'm giving, assume that you can question the premise of what I'm saying, and that it doesn't have to apply to you. I hope I have been helpful in this domain, and I want more of what we want for all of us.

Emotion 7

1. Cognitive Behavioral Therapy, Dialectical Behavior Therapy, Emotional Brain Training
2. Eye Movement Desensitization and Reprocessing

Environment 1

1. Just a quick note here: if you suffer from intrusive thoughts or have any type of diagnosable disordered thinking, the "environment" of silence might not be a safe one for you, and that is completely valid. Please defer to whatever guidance your therapist and/or doctor has given you about how to handle this, and assume I am wrong about your needs here.

Environment 3

1. If this is piquing your interest, read about The Nun Study and the impacts of diet on brain health.

Environment 4

1. But not too much water, of course. As someone who's actually had water poisoning, please don't drink too much water.

   Most of us are not in danger of this. But all you Enneagram 1 people who want to do the right thing, just make sure you don't go to the extreme on this one.

Environment 9

1. And I've coached parents who push back on this advice, and that's also totally fine. As long as they know what they're giving up. I coached a dad recently who said, "I only get ten years with them like this," and I could feel the emotion. He wanted every moment with his kids wanting his attention.

   It turned out, after talking through what he would have to give up to get what he thought he wanted, he didn't want it that much after all. It was a great exercise to remind me, once again, never to make assumptions.

2. Again, assuming they can write.

Environment 11

1. Yes, I meant "hasty." It's an inside joke. If you get it, you get it.
   :)

Progress 7

1. I wrote an entire book on intuition in writers. It's called *Dear Writer, Are You Intuitive?* and if you find yourself struggling with intuition, I highly recommend requesting it from your local library.

Progress 12

1. You hear it, too, don't you? Jason, Jason, Jason…
   Jimmy Rees is my favorite.

Preview Another Becca Syme Book…

1. Credential-wise, I have a Master's degree in Transformational Leadership and am a Gallup-Certified CliftonStrengths® Coach. I teach both on my own platform and on the Margie Lawson Academy, in addition to other places (I've presented at national, regional, and local writing conferences, for one- or two-day workshops). I originally wrote this book as a way for my current students to pass along some of the information they'd learned without making someone commit to the class, because not everyone is a class person, and not everyone needs to take the class.

   But let me say, if you are looking for tips and tricks, or the ten easy steps to success, you are reading the wrong book and should go get your money back right now. This is not a "tips and tricks" book. There are thousands of those out there, and probably better-written than mine would be, because I don't believe that tips and tricks are the way to go.

   So. Even though I talk a fair bit about Write Better-Faster in this book, my purpose is not to get you to take that class. It's to get you to look at your own process and decide for yourself what to quit, what to keep, and what to question.

And then go find one of those "tips and tricks" books we all love so much, and apply what works for you and what doesn't based on the theory in this book.

2. This is as "magic-pill"y as I get, y'all. Enjoy it while it lasts.